MCQs for the MRCP Part 1

With Emphasis on Basic Sciences

H. Kazkaz MRCP
Specialist Registrar in General Medicine and Rheumatology
South Thames Training Programme, UK

K. Mokbel MS, FRCS
Consultant Surgeon
St Bartholomew's Hospital, London, UK

and

M. Sanderson MRCP, MRCGP
General Practitioner
The Spinney Surgery, St Ives, Cambridgeshire, UK

SECOND EDITION

PETROC PRESS

Petroc Press, an imprint of ◆ **Libra**Pharm Limited

Distributors
Plymbridge Distributors Limited, Plymbridge House, Estover Road, Plymouth
PL6 7PZ, UK

Copyright
Original edition © Kluwer Academic Publishers 1993
Reprinted 1996 © LibraPharm Limited
Second edition © LibraPharm Limited 2000

Published in the United Kingdom by
LibraPharm Limited
Gemini House
162 Craven Road
NEWBURY
Berkshire
RG14 5NR
UK

A catalogue record for this book is available from the British Library

ISBN 1 900603 07 1

Typeset by Richard Powell Editorial Services, Basingstoke, RG22 4TX
Printed and bound in the United Kingdom by Grillford Ltd, Milton Keynes

Contents

Introduction to the Second Edition

The MCQ format, as a part of examinations, is here to stay. In an essay assessment, the examiner has to search the paragraphs for relevant facts and opinions, and the examinee can take cover behind the smoke-screen of language.

No such cover is provided by multiple-choice questioning, which not only allows electronic marking, but also offers the candidate a fine stone on which to sharpen the knife of his/her knowledge.

This book has been written primarily for candidates preparing for the MRCP Part 1 examinations who need to assess and revise their knowledge of clinical medicine and applied basic medical sciences. It will also be of great value to postgraduate doctors preparing for the PLAB and MRCGP examinations, and to senior undergraduates. The first edition of this book was published in 1993. It has now been updated so as to keep up with the changes in the MRCP Part 1 examination.

This second edition follows the format of the examination and contains approximately 300 MCQs divided into sections. The emphasis throughout has been on the basic sciences. Explanations to the answers have also been provided to make the MCQ exercise a more useful means of learning.

The relative contribution of each subject towards the MRCP Part 1 examination is as follows:

1. Neurology   9%
2. Cardiology   8%
3. Clinical pharmacology   8%
4. Basic sciences   8%
5. Gastroenterology   7%
6. Haematology   7%
7. Psychiatry   7%
8. Endocrinology   8%
9. Respiratory medicine   7%

How to Use this Book

Each question has a main stem followed by five items each of which must be identified as true **(T)**, false **(F)** or don't know. In the examination, a correct response gains one mark and an incorrect response is penalised by the deduction of one mark. The 'don't know' response gains nothing. The candidate is advised not to spend more than two minutes per question. A score of 50% is regarded as satisfactory.

MCQ Terminology

'usually'   Means more than 50%
'rarely'   Means less than 5%
'never'   Means 0%   ⎫ These terms are not used in
'always'   Means 100%   ⎭ good MCQs
'characteristic'   Refers to a feature which, if absent, would cause the diagnosis to be in doubt
'pathognomonic'   Refers to a feature which is found in that disorder and no other
'associated'   Means more frequently than by chance
'the majority'   Means > 60%

London, July, 2000   H.K.
                                                           K.M.
                                                           M.S.

Multiple-choice Questions

Section 1
Oncology

Q1   Radiotherapy:
A. Cytotoxic effect is decreased in hypoxic cells
B. Causes irreversible DNA damage
C. May cause bone marrow suppression
D. Plays an important role in the treatment of melanoma
E. Has no role in the management of soft tissue sarcoma

Q2   With reference to the cell cycle:
A. RNA and proteins are synthesised during the M phase
B. Duplication of cellular DNA occurs during the S phase
C. The average duration of the cell cycle is approximately 48 hours
D. Mitosis occurs during the G phase
E. Cytotoxic drugs act mainly on resting cells

Q3   RNA oncogenic viruses include:
A. Epstein-Barr virus (EBV)
B. Human papilloma virus (HPV)
C. Human T-cell leukaemia virus (HTLV-1)
D. Hepatitis B virus (HBV)
E. Herpes simplex virus

Q4   Recognised factors for breast cancer include:
A. Multiparity
B. Late menarche
C. Previous oopherectomy
D. Post menopausal obesity
E. Early menopause

Q5   Breast cancer:
A. Due to BRCA1, tends to present in the sixth decade
B. Incidence is increased by premenopausal obesity
C. Screening has reduced mortality in women aged over 50
D. Lifetime risk is approximately 9% in the U.K.
E. Is the leading cause of death among women

Q6   The following tumours commonly metastasise to bone:
A. Renal adenocarcinoma
B. Astrocytoma
C. Carcinoma of the prostate
D. Hepatocellular carcinoma
E. Ductal carcinoma *in situ* of the breast

Q7   The following tumours and appropriate endocrine therapies are correctly paired:
A. Endometrial carcinoma – diethylstilboestrol
B. Phaeochromocytoma – aminoglutathimide
C. Desmoid tumours – tamoxifen
D. Breast carcinoma – aromatase inhibitors
E. Papillary thyroid carcinoma – thyroxine

Q8   The following factors facilitate tumour growth and metastasis:
A. Scatter factor
B. Angiogenesis factor
C. Contact inhibition
D. Matrix metalloproteinases
E. Upregulation of E-cadherins

Q9   Chemotherapy is highly effective in the treatment of:
A. Testicular teratoma
B. Squamous cell carcinoma (SCC) of the anus
C. Malignant melanoma
D. Ovarian carcinoma
E. Gallbladder carcinoma

Q10 Carcinoid tumours:
A. Arise from APUD cells
B. Most frequently arise in the left colon
C. Frequently cause mitral valve stenosis
D. Present with carcinoid syndrome in most cases
E. Can be diagnosed by measuring 5-hydroxyindole acetic acid (5-HIAA) in urine

Q11 Oncogenes:
A. Are genes capable of causing cancer
B. Have been isolated from about 50% of human cancers
C. Products are protein kinases in about 50% of viral oncogenes
D. May uncouple the intranuclear mechanisms involved in growth control from the need for an external stimulus
E. Include growth suppressor genes

Q12 Hyperplasia:
A. Is characteristic of organ enlargement due to inflammation
B. Due to a specific stimulus usually persists even if the stimulus is withdrawn
C. Is the commonest cause of prostatic enlargement
D. Is seen in the myocardium in systemic hypertension
E. Of the parathyroid glands may occur in chronic renal failure

Section 2
Clinical Pharmacology

Q1   Atenolol:
A. Is water insoluble
B. Has more effects on β_2-receptors than β_1-receptors
C. Increases blood flow to the lower limbs
D. Has been shown to reduce the recurrence rate of myocardial infarction
E. Improves glucose tolerance in diabetics

Q2   Angiotensin-converting enzyme (ACE) inhibitors:
A. Are indicated for hypertension in diabetics with nephropathy
B. Improve prognosis in patients with congestive cardiac failure
C. Cause hypokalaemia
D. Improve prognosis in patients with severe bilateral renal artery stenosis
E. Are contraindicated in pregnancy

Q3   Enoxaparin:
A. Is an unfractionated heparin
B. Has a shorter duration of action than conventional heparin
C. Is used in DVT treatment as a subcutaneous injection 1 mg/kg twice daily
D. Is a recognised cause of thrombocytopenia
E. Is used in DVT prophylaxis as a once-daily subcutaneous injection (20 mg)

Q4   Sodium pamidronate:
A. Is absorbed onto hydroxyapatite crystals
B. Increases bone turnover
C. Is effective in treating hypercalcaemia of malignancy
D. Is used in the treatment of multiple myeloma
E. Is available in an oral preparation

Q5　The following drugs are mydriatics:
A. Atropine
B. Tropicamide
C. Cyclopentolate
D. Pilocarpine
E. Carbachol

Q6　The following drugs are contraindicated in chronic simple glaucoma:
A. Topical β-blockers
B. Dorzolamide
C. Latanoprost
D. Topical adrenaline
E. Pilocarpine

Q7　Warfarin:
A. Anticoagulation is effective 24 hours after the first dose
B. Is well absorbed from the alimentary tract
C. Has a half-life of about 6 hours
D. Action is terminated mainly by renal excretion
E. Metabolism by the liver is induced by cimetidine

Q8　Frusemide:
A. Inhibits active chloride reabsorption in the thick segment of the ascending loop of Henle
B. Decreases calcium and magnesium excretion in urine
C. Is to be preferred to thiazides in a patient with a GFR of 12 ml/min
D. Is safely given in combination with gentamicin
E. Is antagonised by indomethacin

Q9　The following statements about insulin are true:
A. Most insulin-dependent diabetics require about 70 units of insulin per day
B. Soluble insulin (acid or neutral) is the only type suitable for intra-venous administration
C. The crystalline form of insulin zinc suspension has an intermediate duration of action (12–16 h)
D. Insulin requirements increase in diabetic patients undergoing major surgery
E. Insulin requirements decrease in bacterial septicaemia as bacteria utilise blood glucose

Q10   The following statements about oral hypoglycaemics are true:

A. Metformin is effective in pancreatectomised animals
B. Sulphonylureas stimulate isolated islets of Langerhans to release insulin *in vitro*
C. Chlorpropramide is the oral hypoglycaemic of choice in a maturity-onset diabetic with heart failure
D. Tolbutamide is to be preferred to chlorpropramide in an elderly patient with renal failure
E. Lactic acidosis is a recognised side effect of phenformin and metformin administration

Q11   Metronidazole:

A. Inhibits alcohol and aldehyde dehydrogenase
B. Impairs the formation of nucleic acids in anaerobic micro-organisms
C. Has been shown to be carcinogenic in humans
D. Has peripheral neuropathy as a recognised side effect
E. Is effective against Entamoeba histolytica

Q12   Carbimazole:

A. Is concentrated in the thyroid gland within minutes of administration
B. Usually renders a thyrotoxic patient euthyroid within 1 week of therapy
C. Is contraindicated in children
D. May cause a sore throat
E. May be combined with thyroxine in the treatment of thyrotoxicosis

Q13   Non-steroidal anti-inflammatory drugs (NSAIDs)

A. Inhibit the enzyme cyclo-oxygenase type 2
B. May cause the closure of a patent ductus arteriosus after birth
C. Reduce gastric acid secretion
D. Potentiate the antihypertensive effect of β-blockers
E. Can inhibit thromboxane synthetase in platelets

Q14   Morphine:

A. Stimulates the chemoreceptor trigger zone
B. Causes histamine release
C. Inhibits the third cranial nerve nucleus
D. Suppresses antidiuretic hormone (ADH) secretion
E. Reduces the tone in the gut wall

Q15   In the treatment of breast cancer, tamoxifen:
A. Decreases the incidence of cancer in the contralateral breast
B. Should not be used in premenopausal patients
C. Is a recognised cause of hypercalcaemia
D. Has been shown to increase survival in node-negative patients
E. Is associated with an increased incidence of endometrial carcinoma

Q16   Omeprazole:
A. Inhibits the hydogen–potassium ATPase (H/K-ATPase) in the secretory canaliculi of the oxyntic cell
B. Has a short duration of action (about 3 hours)
C. Is a recognised cause of hypergastrinaemia
D. Is indicated for grade IV reflux oesophagitis
E. Induces the microsomal enzymes of the liver

Q17   Doses of the following drugs should be reduced in patients with renal impairment:
A. Teicoplanin
B. Tranexamic acid
C. Ranitidine
D. Simvastatin
E. Fluconazole

Q18   Significant amounts of the following drugs are excreted in breast milk:
A. Thiazides
B. Valproate
C. Paracetamol
D. Ciprofloxacin
E. Cimetidine

Q19   The following drugs should be avoided or used with caution in liver disease:
A. Cefuroxime
B. Theophylline
C. Sulphonylureas
D. Suxamethonium
E. Rifampicin

Q20   Phenytoin increases the plasma concentration of the following drugs if given concurrently:
A. Theophylline
B. Digitoxin
C. Cyclosporin
D. Corticosteroids
E. Thyroxine

Q21   Levodopa:
A. Is the amino acid precursor of dopamine
B. Improves tremor more than rigidity in patients with Parkinsonism
C. Is usually given with dopa-carboxylase
D. Improves closed-angle glaucoma
E. Is a recognised cause of peripheral neuropathy

Q22   Recognised indications for penicillamine therapy include:
A. Wilson's disease
B. Lead poisoning
C. Steven's-Johnson syndrome
D. Goodpasture's syndrome
E. Rheumatoid arthropathy

Q23   Recognised adverse effects of zidovudine include:
A. Vitamin B12 deficiency
B. Myelosuppression
C. Pemphigus
D. Renal impairment
E. Hepatic impairment

Q24   5-Fluorouracil:
A. Active metabolites inhibit thymidylate-synthetase
B. Is mostly excreted unchanged in urine
C. Is the most effective chemotherapeutic agent used in the treatment of gastrointestinal adenocarcinoma
D. Requires mesna to reduce its urotoxicity
E. May cause megoblastic anaemia

Q25   Cefuroxime:
A. Is a third generation cephalosporin
B. Has a β-lactam ring
C. Is more effective than ceftriaxone against Gram-positive bacteria
D. Has poor penetration into the CSF
E. Is more effective than ceftazidime against Gram-negative bacteria

Q26   Ranitidine:
A. Blocks gastric H_2 receptors
B. Has a similar half-life to that of cimetidine
C. Is mainly eliminated by hepatic metabolism
D. Blocks androgen receptors
E. Is more effective than omeprazole in the treatment of erosive reflux oesophagitis

Q27   Acyclovir:
A. Is converted to a monophosphate by viral thymidine kinase
B. Activated metabolite is acycloguanosine triphosphate
C. Eradicates herpes simplex virus
D. Is effective topically in the treatment of severe shingles
E. Inhibits reverse transcriptase

Q28   The following anticonvulsants and mechanism of action are correctly paired:
A. Lamotrigine – reduction of GABA synthesis in the brain
B. Vigabatrin – blockade of GABA receptors
C. Phenytoin – reduction of Na^+ flux
D. Carbamazepine – reduction of Na^+ flux
E. Valproate – stimulation of GABA-T enzyme

Q29   Amoxycillin:
A. Is effective against penicillinase-producing bacteria
B. Is better absorbed than ampicillin when given orally
C. Diffuses into Gram-negative bacteria less readily than benzylpenicillin
D. Is effective against most haemophilus influenzae strains
E. Is effective against staphylococcus aureus when combined with clavulanic acid

Q30   The following lipid lowering drugs and mechanism of action are correctly paired:
A. Statins – stimulation of lipoprotein lipase
B. Cholestyramine – anion resin exchange
C. Nicotinic acid – reduction of VLDL release
D. Gemfibrozil – inhibition of HMG COA reductase
E. Colestipol – increased excretion of bile acids

Q31   The following antimicrobial drugs act by inhibiting cell wall synthesis:
A. Ciprofloxacin
B. Trimethoprim
C. Gentamicin
D. Cefuroxime
E. Vancomycin

Q32   Drugs used in the treatment of supraventricular tachycardias include:
A. Lignocaine
B. Adenosine
C. Verapamil
D. Atropine
E. Sotalol

Q33   Stimulation of muscarinic receptors by acetylcholine leads to:
A. Accommodation for near vision
B. Profuse watery salivation
C. Decreased gastrointestinal motility
D. Bronchodilation
E. Hypertension

Q34   Vasodilator drugs include:
A. Losartan
B. Amlodipine
C. Quinidine
D. Milrinone
E. Minoxidil

Q35   Recognised effects of sympathetic-stimulation include:
A. Pupillary constriction
B. Bronchodilatation
C. Increased glycogen synthesis
D. Increased gastrointestinal motility
E. Vasodilatation in skeletal muscle

Q36   Amphotericin:
A. Interacts with ergosterol in the fungal cell wall
B. Is effective against systemic aspergillosis
C. Is not contraindicated in patients with renal failure
D. Formulated in liposomes is less toxic
E. Is well absorbed orally

Q37   The following drugs and corresponding antidotes for overdose are correctly linked:
A. Morphine – naloxone
B. Ferrous sulphate – flumazenil
C. Paracetamol – methionine
D. Carbon monoxide – hyperbaric oxygen
E. Methanol – ethanol

Q38   The following cytotoxic drugs and mechanisms of action are correctly linked:
A. Cytarabine – inhibition of dihydrofolate reductase
B. Fluorouracil – inhibition of thymidylate synthetase
C. Doxorubicin – intercalation between base pairs and blockade of RNA production
D. Methotrexate – formation of covalent cross-links between DNA strands
E. Vincristine – binding to tubulin and destruction of the mitotic spindle

Q39   The adverse effects of corticosteroids include:
A. Pyoderma gangrenosum
B. Hyperkalaemia
C. Avascular necrosis of the femoral head
D. Cataracts
E. Carpel tunnel syndrome

Q40   Aspirin:

A. Is a weak base
B. Metabolites are mainly excreted by the kidneys
C. Is the first line of treatment in patients with rheumatoid arthritis
D. Has been shown to reduce mortality in patients with ischaemic heart disease
E. Increases the incidence of colorectal cancer.

Section 3
Cardiology

Q1   The consequences of biventricular failure include:
A. Increased sympathetic outflow to the failing heart
B. Increased venous pressure
C. Decreased activity of renin–angiotensin–aldosterone system
D. Shifting of normal Starling curve in an upward direction
E. Third heart sound

Q2   Mitral valve prolapse:
A. Is more common in younger women than older women
B. Rarely causes chest pain
C. Is not a predisposing factor to ineffective endocarditis
D. Can lead to cerebral emboli
E. Rarely requires mitral valve replacement

Q3   A loud first heart sound is a feature of:
A. First degree heart block
B. Mitral stenosis
C. Short PR interval
D. Tachycardia (in general)
E. Pericardial effusion

Q4   When the renin-angiotensin aldosterone system is stimulated by a hypovolaemic shock:
A. Renin converts angiotensin I to angiotensin II
B. Angiotensin II causes vasoconstriction of the efferent glomerular arterioles
C. Angiotensin II stimulates the adrenal medulla to synthesise aldosterone
D. Angiotensin II stimulates the adrenal cortex to increase cortisol production
E. Angiotensin converting enzymes degrade bradykinin

Q5 In the management of chronic heart failure:

A. Secondary to severe aortic stenosis, balloon valvoplasty often provides long-lasting symptomatic relief
B. ACE inhibitors are the only vasodilators which have been shown to improve survival
C. Metalazone is useful as adjunctive therapy because it is a potent loop diuretic
D. Angio-oedema may be an adverse effect of ACE inhibitors
E. Long-term digoxin therapy has been shown to provide symptomatic relief only in patients with atrial fibrillation

Q6 Considering the peripheral circulation and blood pressure control:

A. The arterioles account for about 40% of total peripheral resistance
B. Carotid chemoreceptors have no role to play in blood pressure control
C. The central vasomotor centre is situated in the medulla oblongata
D. The sudden assumption of upright posture increases discharge from the carotid and aortic baroreceptors
E. The sudden assumption of upright posture causes constriction of medium-sized veins

Q7 In cardiopulmonary resuscitation:

A. Age is a predictor of outcome
B. Approximately 50% of survivors can expect to leave hospital
C. DC cardioversion should not be attempted if the patient is not connected to a cardiac monitor
D. It is equally satisfactory to give adrenaline down the endotracheal tube or by peripheral vein
E. A satisfactory neurological outcome cannot be obtained if anoxia has been present for more than 10 minutes

Q8 With reference to the ECG:

A. Opening of the aortic valve coincides with the P wave
B. Isovolumetric contraction occurs during the P wave
C. During the ST segment, all parts of ventricles have been depolarised
D. The QT interval is shortened by hypokalaemia
E. During the T wave, the tricuspid valve is normally closed

Q9 Consider the postero-anterior plain film of the chest:

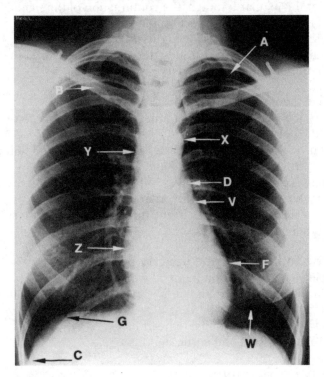

The following statements are correct:

A. 'X' is the aortic knuckle
B. 'Y' is the border of the right atrium
C. 'Z' is the right ventricle
D. 'F' if the left ventricle
E. 'V' is the left atrium

Q10 Cardiac output is decreased in:
A. Systemic arterial hypertension
B. Thyrotoxicosis
C. Hypothermia
D. Moderate anaemia
E. Sinus bradycardia

Q11   The internal jugular vein:
A. Begins at the jugular foramen as a continuation of the sigmoid sinus
B. Passes behind the thoracic duct on the left side
C. Runs alongside the chain of deep cervical lymph nodes
D. Lies medial to the internal carotid artery within the carotid sheath
E. Passes anterior to the phrenic nerve

Q12   The heart:
A. Right atrial appendage projects to the left and overlaps the right side of the aortic root
B. Atrioventricular bundle of His passes through the central fibrous body
C. Coronary arteries are anatomical end arteries
D. The right coronary artery gives off posterior left ventricular wall arteries which appear like an inverted C on angiography
E. The sinus node artery arises from the right coronary artery in about 90% of individuals

Q13   The following are correctly paired:
A. Tricuspid stenosis and prominent 'a' wave
B. Atrial fibrillation and prominent 'a' wave
C. Tamponade and loss of Y descent
D. Cannon 'a' waves and complete heart block
E. Precipitous Y descent and aortic stenosis

Q14   Aortic dissection:
A. Is categorised into two types by the De Bakey classification
B. May present with paraplegia
C. Is always best treated surgically provided the anaesthetic risk is not too great
D. Can be evaluated by magnetic resonance imaging which has a high sensitivity and specificity
E. Can be accurately diagnosed by transoesophageal echocardiography

Q15   Atrial fibrillation:
A. May be precipitated by acute hypovolaemia
B. Which occurs paroxysmally is most effectively prevented by digoxin
C. Of the 'lone' variety, is associated with a particularly high risk of stroke
D. Secondary to thyrotoxicosis is best controlled by β-blockers in the absence of heart failure
E. Is associated with a high risk of stroke if there is a history of a recent onset of congestive cardiac failure

Q16   When considering inserting a pacemaker in the elderly:
A. The commonest reason in patients over 70 years is AV conduction disorders
B. Congestive cardiac failure rarely improves after pacing
C. Digoxin should be ceased if the patient was previously taking it
D. 40% of patients with pacemakers will experience chronotrophic incompetence
E. The commonest presenting symptom requiring pacing is a syncope

Q17   In hypertrophic obstructive cardiomyopathy (HOCM):
A. The ratio of septal to anterior left ventricular wall thickness on echo-cardiography must be at least 1:3
B. A rapid upstroke pulse is only found in about one third of patients
C. There may be mutations in the myosin heavy chain in familial forms
D. There is no improvement in survival with amiodarone
E. The most useful predictor for sudden death is the echocardiographic appearance of the heart

Q18   Congenital heart disease (CHD):
A. Occurs in 10% of live births
B. Risk is increased in patients with Turner's syndrome
C. Is associated with maternal alcohol abuse
D. Characteristically presents with peripheral cyanosis
E. Is a recognised cause of squatting

Q19   The following statements concerning the paediatric electrocardiograph are true:
A. A normal neonatal ECG has an electrical axis of +60° to +80°
B. T waves in V2 lead are upright after 5 years
C. A short PR interval may be seen in glycogen storage disease II
D. Left axis deviation occurs in pulmonary stenosis
E. PR elongation occurs with Ebstein's anomaly

Q20   Renin release is stimulated by:
A. A decrease in blood pressure
B. Propranolol
C. Hyperkalaemia
D. Angiotensin II
E. Salt depletion

Q21   A third heart sound:

A. Is due to rapid atrial filling
B. Is normal at the age of 50 years
C. Occurs just before the first heart sound
D. Is associated with mitral regurgitation
E. Is best heard with the bell of the stethoscope

Q22   Sudden assumption of the upright position initially decreases:

A. Cardiac output
B. Total peripheral resistance
C. Activity of renin–angiotensin–aldosterone system
D. Cerebral PCO_2
E. Heart rate

Section 4

Respiratory Medicine

Q1 **The following are recognised causes of pulmonary disease:**
A. Nebulised pentamidine
B. Amiodarone
C. Sulphasalazine
D. Oral contraceptives
E. Aspirin

Q2 **Legionnaire's disease:**
A. Is a notifiable disease in England and Wales
B. Affects males more commonly than females
C. Normally occurs in outbreaks
D. Has a similar mortality to Pontiac fever
E. Can be caught from whirlpools

Q3 **Obstructive sleep apnoea:**
A. Is a technical term for snoring
B. Affects adults only
C. Is due to episodic pharyngeal collapse
D. Is a recognised risk factor for ischaemic heart disease
E. May be treated with acetazolamide

Q4 **The following are true of pulmonary tuberculosis:**
A. One negative sputum smear is sufficient to demonstrate that a patient is not infectious
B. Smear-positive patients need isolation until acid alcohol-fast bacilli (AAFB) are no longer visible in the sputum
C. It is not a notifiable disease
D. Chemoprophylaxis should be given to all children (aged 0–5) of smear-positive adults
E. It affects 50% of AIDS patients in the U.K.

Q5   With reference to intercostal structures:

A. Transversus thoracis muscle lies between the external and internal intercostal muscles
B. Intercostal neurovascular structures pass behind the superior border of the corresponding rib
C. Anterior intercostal arteries of the first five spaces come off the thoracic aorta
D. Intercostal arteries and nerves lie superficial to the transverse thoracis
E. The first intercostal nerve gives off an anterior cutaneous branch

Q6   With respect to control of respiration:

A. The inspiratory neurones are located in the midbrain
B. Hypoxia increases the firing rate of the carotid bodies
C. Increased arterial PCO_2 increases ventilation mainly by stimulating the central chemoreceptors
D. In metabolic acidosis, H^+ ions increase ventilation mainly by stimulating central chemoreceptors
E. The apneustic centre lies in the upper part of the pons

Q7   The consequences of acute upper airway obstruction include:

A. Cyanosis
B. Bradycardia
C. A rise in blood pH
D. Polycythaemia
E. Respiratory stridor

Q8   The haemoglobin–oxygen dissociation curve is shifted to the right in:

A. Pyrexia
B. Respiratory acidosis
C. States of decreased concentration of 2,3-DPG inside the red cell
D. Polycythaemia
E. Sickle cell anaemia

Q9 In community acquired pneumonias:
A. The commonest pathogen is *Mycoplasma pneumoniae*
B. Erythromycin is the first line antibiotic for psittacosis
C. Serum urea correlates with the severity of the illness
D. Ciprofloxacin can be used as a single agent when the organism is not known
E. The pneumococcal antigen can be identified in urine

Q10 In asthma:
A. The neutrophil is the main mediator of the inflammatory response
B. There is a progressive decline in lung function over a number of years
C. Mortality is declining
D. Reduction of inspiratory flow can be demonstrated on a flow-volume loop
E. Inhaled steroids should be prescribed if more than occasional use of inhaled salbutamol is required.

Q11 The diagnosis of cryptogenic organising pneumonitis (COP) is:
A. Supported by the finding of patent alveolar ducts in lung biopsy
B. Associated with rheumatoid arthritis
C. Aided by bronchoalveolar lavage (BAL)
D. Possible by serological tests
E. Excluded if there is no prompt response to steroids

Q12 Recognised causes of acute stridor in children include:
A. Hypocalcaemia
B. Infectious mononucleosis
C. Laryngomalacia
D. Laryngotracheobronchitis
E. C_1 esterase inhibitor deficiency

Q13 Chronic lung disease of prematurity (bronchopulmonary dysplasia)
A. May be diagnosed as oxygen dependence beyond two months
B. Is due to surfactant deficiency
C. Ventilator dependency may be reduced by the use of dexamethasone
D. May be complicated by urea-plasma infection
E. Is associated with gastro-oesophageal reflux

Q14   A honeycomb lung is a recognised feature of:
A. Neurofibromatosis
B. Sarcoidosis
C. Tuberose sclerosis
D. Trichitillomania
E. Systemic sclerosis

Q15   Sarcoidosis:
A. Is the commonest cause of erythema nodosum
B. Affects the skin in 60% of cases
C. Is commonly complicated by hypocalcaemia
D. Carries a better prognosis in black races
E. Is usually associated with reduced serum levels of angiotensin converting enzyme

Q16   In respiratory acidosis:
A. PCO_2 is raised
B. Blood pH is raised
C. Serum bicarbonate is reduced
D. Papilloedema may occur
E. Bicarbonate is the treatment of choice

Q17   Recognised features of asbestosis include:
A. Finger clubbing
B. Cor pulmonale
C. Pulmonary fibrosis
D. Progression of disease 20 years after exposure
E. Increased carbon monoxide transfer factor

Q18   Adult respiratory distress syndrome (ARDS)
A. Is characterised by an increased pulmonary capillary wedge pressure (PCWP)
B. Increases lung compliance
C. Is a recognised complication of septicaemia
D. Is a recognised complication of blood transfusion
E. Usually responds to corticosteroids

Q19 The following are recognised manifestations of bronchial carcinoma:
A. Hypertrophic pulmonary osteoarthropathy
B. Goodpasture's syndrome
C. Secondary hyperparathyroidism
D. Peripheral neuropathy
E. Acanthosis nigricans

Q20 The characteristic clinical features of acute hypoxaemic (type 1) respiratory failure includes:
A. Hypoxia
B. Tachypnoea
C. Large tidal volume
D. Shifting of the haemoglobin-oxygen dissociation curve to the left
E. Arterial $PCO_2 > 8\,kPa$

Q21 The diagnosis of ARDS is based on:
A. Refractory hypoxaemia
B. Bilateral pulmonary infiltrates on x-ray
C. Lung compliance $> 30\,ml/cm\ H_2O$
D. Pulmonary artery occlusion pressure $> 15\,mmHg$
E. Hypercapnia

Section 5
Gastroenterology

Q1 Acute pancreatitis:
A. Is idiopathic in more than 60% of cases
B. Is a recognised side-effect of carbamazepine therapy
C. May be caused by ascariasis
D. Secondary to alcohol has a higher mortality rate than for gallstone-associated pancreatitis
E. Is a risk factor for the development of pancreatic carcinoma

Q2 In irritable bowel syndrome:
A. Women and men are equally affected
B. The symptoms can be produced by balloon distension of the rectum in a small number of patients
C. Cisapride may accelerate colonic transit and may improve constipation
D. Bloating can be exacerbated by fatty acids in some individuals
E. Colonic transit times are longer in patients where diarrhoea predominates

Q3 The oesophagus:
A. Lower third lymphatic drainage ends in the coeliac lymph nodes
B. Is a site for portal-systemic anastomosis at its lower third
C. Thoracic part lies anterior to the left recurrent laryngeal nerve
D. Is constricted by the left bronchus
E. Lower third is the commonest site for carcinoma of the oesophagus

Q4 Porto-systemic anastomoses occur in the following sites:
A. Around the umbilicus
B. The middle third of the oesophagus
C. The lower end of the rectum
D. The bare area of the liver
E. The appendix

Q5 Vasoactive intestinal polypeptide (VIP)

A. Is secreted by non-beta islet cells in the pancreas
B. Stimulates gastric acid secretion
C. Enhances small intestinal reabsorption of water and electrolytes
D. Normal serum level is approximately 3000 pg/ml
E. May be secreted by a bronchogenic carcinoma

Q6 The following statements concern bilirubin and its metabolites:

A. The daily production of bilirubin in a 70 kg adult is about 300 mg
B. The conjugation of bilirubin is performed by the β-glucuronidase enzymes
C. The conjugated bilirubin is secreted into the bile by simple diffusion
D. A fraction of urobilinogen is re-absorbed from the intestine and re-excreted through the liver
E. Urobilins are colourless compounds

Q7 The following are true of primary biliary cirrhosis:

A. The clinical and biochemical state of the patient correlates well with the severity of histological changes in the liver
B. It is associated with Sjögren's syndrome
C. A rising bilirubin level is the most important indicator of a poor prognosis
D. Ursodeoxycholic acid has been shown to improve biochemical abnormalities in primary biliary cirrhosis
E. It does not recur in patients treated with liver transplantation

Q8 Ulcerative colitis:

A. May spare the rectum
B. Presents most commonly in the over 40s
C. Has a recognised association with fibrosing alveolitis
D. Can be cured by proctocolectomy
E. Should not be treated with sulphazalazine in women trying to start a family

Q9 The following are true of gallstones:

A. Pigment stones may occur in thalassaemia
B. Oestrogens may cause gallstones
C. In the over 60s, gallstones are commoner in men than women
D. The majority of patients with gallbladder cancer also have gallstones
E. Calcified gallstones may be dissolved using methyl tert-butyl ether

Q10   Histopathological features of a jejunal biopsy in coeliac disease include:
A. Glandular hypoplasia
B. Subtotal villous atrophy
C. Lymphoid infiltration of the lamina propria
D. Crypt hyperplasia
E. Epithelioid granuloma

Q11   Gastric acid secretion is suppressed by:
A. Histamine
B. H_1 blockers
C. Gastrin inhibiting polypeptide (GIP)
D. Atropine
E. Gastrin

Q12   With respect to bile:
A. About two litres of bile are secreted into the duodenum daily
B. Most of the bile acids are reabsorbed in the colon
C. Some of the urobilinogen absorbed in the colon is excreted in the urine
D. The solubility of cholesterol in the bile is independent of its relative molar concentration
E. Cholecystokinin-pancreozymin causes bile secretion into the duodenum

Q13   Pancreatic secretion may be stimulated by:
A. Gastrin
B. Secretin
C. Atropine
D. Cholecystokinin-pancreozymin (CCK-PZ)
E. Vasoactive intestinal polypeptide (VIP)

Q14   The following transmitter substances increase intestinal secretion of water and electrolytes:
A. Noradrenaline
B. VIP (vasoactive intestinal polypeptide)
C. Prostaglandins
D. Dihydroxy bile acids
E. Acetylcholine

Q15 In the digestion and absorption of fat:
A. The mixed micelle formed is water soluble
B. Vitamins K, D, A and E are packaged into the chylomicrons within the enterocytes
C. Most of the chylomicrons pass from the enterocytes into the portal vein.
D. Deficiency of apoprotein B synthesis causes fat malabsorption
E. Long-chain triglycerides are more water-soluble than medium-chain triglycerides (MCTs)

Q16 Obstructive jaundice usually:
A. Raises the serum level of conjugated bilirubin
B. Reduces prothrombin time (PT)
C. Increases urinary excretion of urobilinogen
D. Causes dark urine and pale stools
E. Elevates the serum level of alkaline phosphatase

Q17 The following are commoner in Crohn's disease than in ulcerative colitis:
A. Crypt abscesses in the bowel mucosa
B. Pseudopolyps in the bowel lumen
C. The development of carcinoma as a complication
D. Bowel obstruction as a complication
E. Involvement of the submucosa and deeper layers

Q18 Cholesterol gallstones:
A. Are usually multiple, small and hard
B. Do not form in bile that contains a molar concentration of cholesterol of about 30%
C. Are a recognised complication of diabetes mellitus
D. May be visible on a plain abdominal x-ray
E. Commonly develop in long standing haemolytic anaemias

Q19 The consequences of chronic liver disease include:
A. Hypergammaglobulinaemia
B. Hypoalbuminaemia
C. Encephalopathy
D. Low plasma levels of Factor VIII
E. Gynaecomastia

Q20   The gastro-intestinal complications of AIDS include:

A. Colitis due to cytomegalovirus
B. Diarrhoea and superficial ulcers due to *Mycobacterium avium intra-cellulare*
C. Chronic perianal herpes simplex
D. *Salmonella enterocolitis*
E. Kaposi's sarcoma

Q21   Consider the following CT scan of the abdomen (post-contrast film):

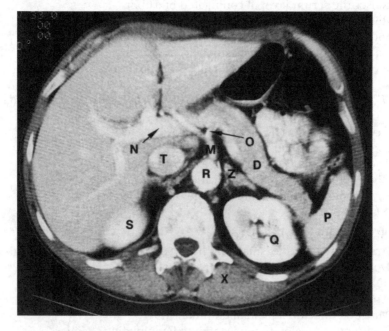

The following statements are correct:

A. 'N' is the main portal vein
B. 'M' is the common bile duct
C. 'P' is the left kidney
D. 'T' is the inferior vena cava
E. This cut lies at the level of the second lumbar vertebra

Q22   The following are recognised causes of pancreatitis:
A. Pancreatic cancer
B. Hypocalcaemia
C. Excessive alcohol intake
D. Budd-Chiari syndrome
E. Cystic fibrosis

Q23   The consequences of resection of the terminal ileum include:
A. Subacute combined degeneration of the spinal cord
B. Diarrhoea
C. Decreased incidence of gallstone formation
D. Iron deficiency anaemia
E. Peripheral neuropathy

Q24   The following tests are used in the diagnosis of chronic pancreatitis:
A. Pentagastrin test
B. Lundh test
C. Secretin test
D. Bentiromide test
E. Fluorescein dilaurate test

Q25   *Helicobacter pylori* infections are detected by:
A. Gastric pH monitoring
B. Gastric biopsy and microscopy
C. Gastric biopsy and culture
D. Gastric biopsy and urease activity
E. Serology

Q26   Fibre optic upper digestive endoscopy:
A. Is less accurate than video endoscopy
B. Is superior to barium meal examination
C. Replaces the need for small bowel biopsy capsules in coeliac disease
D. Has no mortality
E. Usually requires IV sedation which may be reversed with flumazenil

Q27   Mortality in patients with gastrointestinal haemorrhage:

A. Is low under 65 years
B. Is definitely reduced by vigorous antacid therapy
C. Relates mainly to associated diseases
D. Is higher in oesophageal variceal bleeding
E. Is higher in Mallory–Weiss tears

Q28   Acute fulminant hepatic failure (FHF) commonly results in:

A. Hyperglycaemia
B. Hyperkalaemia
C. Asteraxis
D. Lactic acidosis
E. Increased total body sodium

Section 6
Neurology and Psychiatry

Q1   The electromyogram (EMG)

A. Records the electrical activity of muscle fibres making up the motor units
B. Records the magnitude of muscle contraction
C. Shows regular electrical activity when healthy muscle is relaxed
D. Can be recorded by placing the electrode on the skin overlying the muscle
E. Shows fibrillation potentials in denervated muscle

Q2   The following figure represents an action potential recorded from an unmyelinated axon:

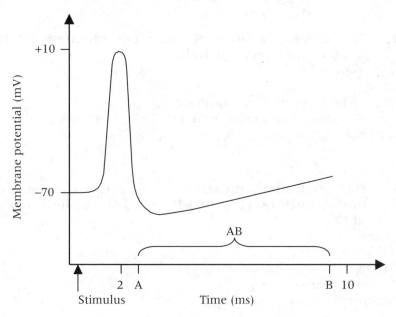

A. During the period AB (hyperpolarisation) the Na^+ channels are more active than the K^+ channels
B. During AB a strong current (stimulus) is needed to generate another action potential
C. More ionic exchange (across the membrane) occurs in this unmyelinated axon than in a myelinated axon
D. The greater the diameter of the axon the greater the conduction velocity of this action potential
E. Saltatory conduction is a feature of conduction in unmyelinated axons

Q3   The clinical features of an injury to the common peroneal nerve due to a fracture of the neck of the fibular include:
A. Paralysis of tibialis anterior
B. Positive Trendelenburg test
C. Paralysis of peroneus longus
D. Equinovarus deformity of the foot
E. Calcaneovalgus deformity of the foot

Q4   The clinical features of complete aparalysis of the third cranial nerve include:
A. Pupil constriction
B. Ptosis
C. The eye looks laterally and downward
D. Loss of consensual light reflex (light is shone in the affected eye)
E. Loss of accommodation reflex

Q5   Damage to the sympathetic nerves from the thoracolumbar outflow (T11 to L2) will disturb the function of the:
A. Detrusor muscle
B. Bladder neck
C. Trigone
D. External sphincter
E. Seminar vesicles

Q6   A complete division of the femoral nerve results in:
A. Foot drop
B. Paraesthesia of the lateral aspect of the foot
C. Failure of knee extension
D. Sensory loss over the medial part of the lower leg
E. Failure of adduction of the thigh at the hip joint

Q7   The cerebral blood flow
A. Accounts for about 15% of the cardiac output
B. Is decreased by hypocapnia
C. Is decreased by hypoxia
D. Is mainly controlled by sympathetic and parasympathetic mechanism
E. Is increased by isoflurane in general anaesthesia

Q8   Injury to the medial cord of the brachial plexus results in:
A. Paralysis of all the intrinsic muscles of the hand
B. Loss of elbow flexion
C. Loss of cutaneous sensations over the anterior surface of palm and fingers
D. Paralysis of the long flexors of the fingers
E. Paralysis of the pronator teres

Q9   The facial nerve:
A. Gives off the chorda tympani nerve 5 mm below the stylomastoid foramen
B. If injured along its vertical course within the mastoid bone, the stapedius reflex would be normal
C. Has a mandibular branch which passes about 2.5 cm behind the angle of the mandible
D. Supplies secretomotor fibres to the submandibular gland
E. In the bony wall of the middle ear, lies posterior to the mastoid antrum and air cells

Q10   The stretch reflex pathway consists of:
A. Spindle primary endings
B. Golgi tendon organs
C. Small-diameter afferents (0.5–70 m/s)
D. Monosynaptic excitatory synapses onto the antagonistic motor neurons
E. Monosynaptic excitatory synapses onto motor neurons innervating the same muscle

Q11   The blood–brain barrier (BBB)
A. Contains endothelial cells which have tight junctions
B. Allows transport of substances in one direction only, i.e. out of the vascular system into the brain
C. Allows water to cross by simple diffusion
D. Contains astrocytic foot processes
E. Lacks mitochondria in the endothelial cells

Q12   The normal CSF contains:
A. About 50 polymorphs per mm^3
B. Oligoclonal bands in 50% of cases
C. 0.2–0.4 mg of protein per litre
D. Immunoglobulins (IgG)
E. A concentration of glucose less than one third that of blood

Q13   The following statements concern membrane potential:
A. If one electrode is inserted into the axon (the other is earthed), the cathode ray oscilloscope shows a positive potential of the inside relative to the outside
B. The resting membrane potential is about –65 mV
C. The internal potential is directly proportional to the logarithm of the potassium concentration outside the membrane
D. The Na^+:K^+ ratio is 3:2 in all cells
E. The resting potential undergoes a transient depolarisation to generate the action potential

Q14   The synaptic potential:
A. Channel is voltage-gated
B. Na^+ and K^+ currents are simultaneous
C. In the post-synaptic membrane, is inhibitory when depolarising
D. Is also called a graded potential
E. In the post-synaptic membrane, is excitatory when GABA binds to the post-synaptic receptor

Q15   Sodium channels:
A. Open within 1 ms upon depolarisation
B. Remain open as long as depolarisation is maintained
C. Are least dense in the nodes of Ranvier
D. Consist of polypeptide chains
E. Open in response to tetrodotoxin

Q16   The clinical features of transient ischaemic attacks (TIAs) affecting the carotid system include:

A. Aphasia
B. Ataxia
C. Dysarthria
D. Amaurosis fugax
E. Hemiparesis

Q17   The spinothalamic tracts of the spinal cord transmit the following sensory modalities:

A. Pain
B. Two point discrimination
C. Joint position
D. Temperature
E. Vibration

Q18   The following cutaneous areas and supplying sensory nerve roots are correctly paired:

A. The sole of the foot – S3
B. The little finger – T1
C. The groin – L5
D. The umbilicus – T10
E. The index finger – C5

Q19   The following statements refer to brain circulation:

A. The posterior cerebral artery arises from the internal carotid
B. The lateral surface of each cerebral hemisphere is supplied mainly by the anterior cerebral artery
C. The posterior cerebral artery gives rise to the posterior inferior cerebellar (PIC) artery
D. The middle cerebral artery supplies the internal capsule via penetrating branches
E. The inferior petrosal sinus drains into the transverse sinus

Q20   The median nerve:

A. Derives its fibres from segments C6–C8 and T1
B. Gives off a muscular branch to the triceps
C. Supplies the ulnar half of the flexor digitorum profundus
D. Supplies the third and fourth lumbricals
E. Gives off sensory branches to the dorsal aspects of the lateral 2½ fingers

Q21　The radial nerve:

A. Derives its fibres from segments C6–C8 and T1
B. Gives off a muscular branch to the biceps
C. Gives off sensory branches to the dorsal aspects of the radial half of the hand
D. Accompanies the profunda artery during its descent in the arm
E. Supplies the anoconeus

Q22　The following autonomic neurons are adrenergic:

A. The postganglion sympathetic neurons to the small bowel
B. The postganglion sympathetic neurons to the sweat gland
C. Some preganglionic neurons
D. Anatomically sympathetic vasodilator neurons to skeletal muscle blood vessels
E. The postganglionic parasympathetic neurons to the stomach

Q23　Cholinergic impulses in the autonomic nervous system produce:

A. A decrease in atrial contractility
B. Detrusor muscle relaxation
C. Ciliary muscle contraction
D. Gallbladder relaxation
E. Ejaculation

Q24　The following drugs are miotics:

A. Pilocarpine
B. Neostigmine
C. Atropine
D. Cocaine
E. Carbachol

Q25　The ulnar nerve supplies the following muscles in the hand:

A. Adductor pollicis
B. All dorsal interossei
C. The lateral two lumbricals
D. Abductor pollicis brevis
E. All hypothenar muscles

Q26 The spinal cord:

A. Subdural space contains the cerebrospinal fluid (CSF)
B. Segment T12 lies at the level of vertebral body T11
C. Transmits two-point discrimination sense in the lateral white column
D. Hemisection results in contralateral upper motor neuron paralysis below the level of the lesion
E. Hemisection results in contralateral loss of pain and temperature sense below the lesion

Q27 The clinical features of a lumbar disc prolapse affecting root S1 only include:

A. Paraesthesia on the medial aspect of the foot
B. A positive femoral stretch
C. Weakness and wasting of dorsiflexors of the foot
D. Limitation of straight leg raising
E. Imparied knee jerk

Q28 Aneurysmal subarachnoid haemorrhage (SAH)

A. Has a 20% risk of recurrence in the first month following the initial bleed
B. Has a recurrence rate of 15% per year six months following the initial bleed
C. May be complicated by inappropriate ADH secretion
D. Is associated with increased levels of circulating catecholamines
E. Has a better short-term prognosis than SAH of unknown cause

Q29 The following are recognised neurological features of HIV infection:

A. Distal symmetric sensorimotor neuropathy
B. Progressive myelopathy
C. Subacute encephalopathy
D. Cranial neuropathy
E. Retinopathy

Q30 A high stepping gait is a feature of:

A. Peroneal muscular atrophy
B. Parkinson's disease
C. Lesions of the cerebellar vermis
D. Polyneuropathy
E. Common peroneal nerve palsy

Q31   The following muscular dystrophies are dominantly inherited:
A. Limb-girdle dystrophy
B. Facio-scapulo-humeral dystrophy
C. Becker's muscular dystrophy
D. Myotonic dystrophy
E. Duchenne's muscular dystrophy

Q32   Loss of position and vibration sense alone is common in:
A. Tabes dorsalis
B. Friedreich's ataxia
C. Familial calcification of the basal ganglia (Fahr's disease)
D. Subacute combined degeneration of the cord (SCDC)
E. Amyotrophic lateral sclerosis

Q33   The following are associated with benign intracranial hypertension:
A. Addison's disease
B. Galactosaemia
C. Young slim males
D. Behçet's syndrome
E. Vitamin A deficiency

Q34   The following lipid storage disorders and the enzyme defects are correctly paired:
A. Tay-Sachs disease – hexosaminidase A
B. Neimann-Pick disease (type A) – spingomyelinase
C. Farber's lipogranulomatosis – arylsulphatase
D. Gaucher's disease (adult type) – sphingomyelinase
E. Metachromatic leukodystrophy – hexosaminidase

Q35   The following are recognised clinical features of right cerebral astrocytoma:
A. Right hemiplegia
B. Bradycardia
C. Papilloedema
D. Generalised convulsions
E. Right sixth nerve palsy

Q36 Kurt Schneider's first rank symptoms include:
A. Thought withdrawal
B. Secondary delusions
C. Disturbance of memory
D. Auditory hallucinations
E. Nihilism

Q37 The usual clinical features of major depressive illness include:
A. Visual hallucinations
B. Grandiose delusions of power
C. Feelings of unworthiness
D. Primary delusions
E. Clouding of consciousness

Q38 The following features are typical of mania:
A. Hyperactivity
B. Elevated mood
C. Flight of ideas
D. Memory disturbances
E. Somatic passivity

Q39 Alcohol abuse is associated with:
A. Wernicke–Korsakoff's syndrome
B. Farber's disease
C. Phobias
D. Pathological jealousy
E. Dilated cardiomyopathy

Q40 Cocaine addiction:
A. Accounts for 40% of new notifications for drug misuse in the UK
B. Is associated with fatal cardiac dysrhythmias
C. May cause perforation of the nasal septum
D. Is a recognised cause of depression
E. Craving is increased by fluoxetine administration

Section 7
Endocrinology

Q1   Cortisol:
A. Synthesis by the adrenals is controlled by ACTH via cyclic AMP
B. Reduces gluconeogenesis
C. Plasma level reaches a maximum at about midnight
D. Has considerable mineralocorticoid activity
E. Enhances production of angiotensinogen

Q2   The following factors stimulate ADH (vasopressin) secretion:
A. Exercise
B. Hyperglycaemia
C. Severe hypovolaemia
D. Decreased plasma osmolarity
E. Pain

Q3   Recognised causes of hyperprolactinaemia include:
A. Bromocriptine
B. Hypothyroidism
C. Adrenal insufficiency
D. Cimetidine
E. Dopamine

Q4   Regarding Vasopressin (ADH)
A. Vasopressin is synthesised in the posterior pituitary gland
B. Deficiency leads to a risk of water intoxication
C. Excessive secretion usually results in diabetes insipidus (DI)
D. The primary physiological stimulus for vasopressin secretion is increased plasma osmolarity
E. Vasopressin acts mainly on the distal convoluted tubules and collecting ducts of the kidney

Q5 Human growth hormone (hGH)
A. Is synthesised by basophilic cells in the anterior pituitary
B. Secretion is stimulated by a rise in blood glucose concentration
C. Has growth-related effects that are primarily mediated by somato-medin
D. Secretion is inhibited by somatostatin
E. Increases protein synthesis

Q6 The principal actions of insulin include:
A. Increased lipolysis in adipose tissue
B. Increased ketogenesis in the liver
C. Increased glucose uptake by muscle and adipose tissue
D. Decreased glycogen synthesis
E. Increased protein synthesis

Q7 With respect to the thyroid gland:
A. The thyroid gland selectively concentrates iodine from plasma iodide
B. Thyroid stimulating hormone (TSH) is secreted by acidophil cells in the anterior pituitary gland
C. Gland vascularity and cellularity is increased by TSH
D. Thyroxine (T4) has a half-life of 12 hours
E. T4 produces effects within 6 hours of secretion

Q8 The effects of glucocorticoids include:
A. Increasing prostaglandin synthesis
B. Decreasing the number of circulating leukocytes
C. Increasing the delivery of amino acids to the liver to increase glucose production
D. Suppression of the immune response
E. Potassium reabsorption in the distal renal tubule

Q9 The action of antidiuretic hormone (ADH) includes:
A. Reduction of cardiac output
B. An increase in total peripheral resistance
C. Decreased release of ACTH
D. Increased renal reabsorption of sodium
E. Decreased release of factor VIII

Q10   Luteinising hormone release hormone (LHRH)
A. Has a constant secretion rate throughout the day
B. Controls the secretion of TSH
C. Analogues may be used in the treatment of prostatic carcinoma
D. May be used in the treatment of infertility in both sexes
E. Produces a greater response in LH release when given intravenously during the early follicular phase rather than during the luteal phase

Q11   Testosterone causes:
A. An increase in scalp hair
B. Positive nitrogen balance
C. Decrease in body hair
D. The epiphyses of long bones to unite
E. Increased pituitary secretion of luteinising hormone (LH)

Q12   The clinical features of Cushing's syndrome include:
A. Vascular calcification
B. Hirsutism
C. Diabetes mellitus
D. Increased libido
E. Aortic stenosis

Q13   The clinical features of Addison's disease include:
A. Hypertension
B. Hyperpigmentation of skin creases
C. Hyperkalaemia
D. Hirsutism
E. Hypercalcaemia

Q14   21-Hydroxylase deficiency is:
A. Inherited in an autosomal recessive fashion
B. Due to a gene mutation on chromosome 5
C. Less common than 11-hydroxylase deficiency
D. Characterised by hypokalaemia
E. Treated by metysapone

Q15   Grave's disease:

A. Is due to antibodies to thyroglobulin
B. Is more common in women
C. Presents most commonly in the second decade
D. May be treated with radioactive iodine
E. Is characterised by increased levels of TSH

Section 8
Nephrology

Q1   In the nephron of a healthy kidney:
A. The descending loop of Henle is impermeable to water
B. Almost all the filtered protein is reabsorbed in the proximal convoluted tubule
C. ADH renders the cells lining the collecting ducts permeable to water
D. In the distal tubule, further Na^+ is reabsorbed while K^+ and H^+ are secreted under the influence of ADH (vasopressin)
E. All the filtered glucose is re-absorbed in the proximal tubule

Q2   Common consequences of chronic renal failure (CRF) include:
A. Metabolic acidosis
B. Hypercalcaemia
C. Normochromic normocytic anaemia
D. Hypokalaemia
E. Primary hyperparathyroidism

Q3   Microalbuminuria:
A. Is defined as the passage of small particles of albumin in urine which is not otherwise detectable by Albustix
B. Is a predictor of death from cardiovascular disease only in the diabetic population
C. In an insulin-dependent diabetic patient is almost always associated with proliferative retinopathy
D. Has been shown to be significantly reduced by strict glycaemic control in insulin dependent diabetic patients
E. Is present in 30% of patients with newly diagnosed insulin-dependent diabetes mellitus.

Q4   In the nephrotic syndrome:

A. Both serum total cholesterol and triglycerides are usually elevated
B. Serum HDL cholesterol tends to be reduced
C. Occurring in a diabetic patient, diabetic nephropathy is rarely the underlying cause for the heavy proteinuria
D. Patients should be encouraged to have a very high dietary protein intake in order to compensate for the marked proteinuria
E. Renal vein thrombosis is a recognised complication

Q5   Diabetic nephropathy:

A. Often develops within 5 years of the onset of insulin-dependent DM
B. Has a declining incidence 20 years after the onset of IDDM
C. May be predicted by the development of microalbuminuria
D. Is associated with the same mortality as other causes of end-stage renal failure
E. May be retarded by appropriate antihypertensive therapy

Q6   The following provide a reasonably good assessment of GFR:

A. Serum albumin
B. Serum creatinine
C. Serum B_2-microglobulin
D. Water deprivation test
E. Aminoacid chromatography on urine

Q7   In renovascular hypertension:

A. Isotope renography will identify 90% of renal artery stenoses
B. Due to atherosclerosis, renal failure is an uncommon consequence In the elderly population
C. Successful treatment of the hypertension by angioplasty in more likely to occur in cases of fibromuscular dysplasia rather than atherosclerosis
D. The ratio of peripheral to renal renin activity is a useful predictor of outcome in patients who are being considered for vascular reconstruction
E. Loop diuretics are particularly useful in the medical management

Q8   Renin release is stimulated by:

A. A decrease in blood pressure
B. Propranolol
C. An increase in plasma K^+ concentration
D. Angiotensin II
E. Salt depletion

Q9   Abnormal colour of urine is a feature of:

A. Rifampicin therapy
B. Cystinuria
C. Phenylketonuria
D. Congenital porphyria
E. Phaeochromocytoma

Q10   Serum potassium levels may be reduced by:

A. Hyperventilation
B. Intravenous sodium bicarbonate
C. Nebulised salbutamol
D. Calcium exchange resins
E. Atenolol

Section 9

Rheumatology and Immunology

Q1   Human leukocyte antigens (HLA)
A. Genes are located on the short arm of chromosome 6
B. Class II are controlled by A, B and C loci
C. Compatibility is more crucial to graft survival than BO blood group compatibility
D. Matching at the A and C loci has the greatest influence on graft survival
E. Can be identified by incubating donor lymphocytes with HLA typing sera

Q2   The following statements concerning gout are correct:
A. Gout is unusual in women prior to the menopause
B. Gout may be associated with hereditary renal tubular disorders
C. Serum uric acid is diagnostic of the disease
D. The dose of allopurinol needs to be reduced in renal impairment to avoid toxicity
E. The acute phase of gout is best treated with allopurinol

Q3   In Behçet's disease:
A. Presentation occurs most commonly in the fifth to sixth decade
B. Renal impairment is common
C. Dural sinus thrombosis may occur
D. Myocardial infarction is a recognised complication
E. Thalidomide is effective in the treatment of severe recurrent aphthous stomatitis.

Q4   Dermatomyositis and polymyositis:

A. Are more common in men than women
B. Produce muscle weakness more commonly than muscle tenderness
C. Both commonly produce arthralgia
D. Associated with interstitial lung disease, are related to the presence of the anti-Jo-1 antibody
E. Both show capillary damage on muscle histology

Q5   Recognised causes of osteoporosis include:

A. Hormone replacement therapy
B. Previous oopherectomy
C. Excessive alcohol consumption
D. Heparin
E. Previous orchidectomy

Q6   In the treatment of osteoporosis:

A. Oestrogens acts directly on bone cells via high-affinity oestrogen receptors
B. Raloxifene reduces the risk of osteoporosis
C. Bisphosphonates act by inhibiting bone resorption
D. Etridonate should only be given on an intermittent basis because long-term continuous treatment leads to impairment of newly synthesised bone matrix.
E. Sodium fluoride may produce a lower extremity pain syndrome.

Q7   The following are true of slow-acting antirheumatic drugs (SAARDs)

A. Oral gold has been shown to be as effective as penicillamine and sulphasalazine
B. Among the SAARDs, intramuscular gold is the most likely to be stopped because of toxicity
C. Sulphasalazine may cause a leucopenia
D. Thrombocytopenia associated with penicillamine therapy is an idiosyncratic side-effect
E. Patients treated with methotrexate should be advised not to take concomitant cotrimoxazole therapy

Q8   Women with systemic lupus erythematosus (SLE)
A. Are at no increased risk of miscarriage
B. Usually give birth to children with at least one abnormality
C. Have an increased risk of giving birth to children with congenital heart block
D. May take chloroquine safely in pregnancy
E. Have active disease if their ESR is elevated in pregnancy

Q9   Pauci-articular juvenile chronic arthritis:
A. Is more common in females
B. Occurs predominantly in late childhood
C. Is erosive at small hand joints
D. Is defined by the involvement of four or less joints
E. Is associated with uveitis if antinuclear serology is negative

Q10   The following are examples of antibody-dependent cytotoxic hypersensitivity:
A. Hyperthyroidism in Grave's disease
B. Haemolytic anaemia due to Mycoplasma pneumoniae
C. Haemolysis following blood transfusion
D. The main mechanism mediating acute early rejection of a transplanted kidney
E. Hyperacute rejection of a transplanted kidney

Q11   Cell mediated immunity reactions are:
A. Dependent on complement
B. Independent of antibody
C. Dependent on T-lymphocytes
D. Usually increased in AIDS patients
E. Responsible for autoimmune haemolytic anaemia

Q12   Psoriatic arthropathy:
A. Is commonest in Japan
B. Is a sero-negative arthropathy
C. Usually spares the terminal phalangeal joint
D. May take the form of arthritis mutilans
E. Is successfully treated with chloroquine

Q13   The clinical features of polymyositis–dermatomyositis complex include:

A. Low levels of phosphokinase(CPK) in serum
B. Polyarthritis
C. Waddling gait
D. Nikolisky's sign
E. A heliotrope rash around the eyes

Q14   The clinical features of systemic lupus erythematous include:

A. Loss of hair
B. Raynaud's phenomenon
C. Telengectasia at the base of the nail
D. Photosensitivity
E. Subcutaneous nodules

Q15   Progressive systemic sclerosis:

A. Typically presents after the age of 60 years
B. Is associated with primary biliary sclerosis
C. Has an overall five-year survival rate of 10%
D. Is more common than SLE
E. Affects the gastrointestinal tract in the majority of cases

Q16   Recognised causes of Raynaud's phenomenon include:

A. Systemic sclerosis
B. Buerger's disease
C. Vinyl chloride poisoning
D. Syringomyelia
E. Nifedipine

Q17   Rheumatoid arthritis:

A. Has a 50% concordance rate in identical twins
B. Risk is reduced in patients with HLA-DR4 tissue type
C. Disease activity correlates with titres of rheumatoid factor
D. May cause Caplan's syndrome
E. Is a recognised cause of pulmonary hypertension

Q18 **The following are features of polymyalgia rheumatica:**

A. Elevated CPK levels

B. Abnormal EMG

C. Elevated ESR

D. True muscle weakness

E. Resolution of symptoms within 72 hours of oral steroids administration

Section 10

Dermatology and Genitourinary Medicine

Q1   The following dermatoses typically affect the trunk:
A. Pityriasis rosea
B. Pityriasis versicolor
C. Keratoderma blennorrhagicum
D. Guttate psoriasis
E. Acute pompholyx

Q2   Dermatitis herpetiformis:
A. Is associated with gastrointestinal symptoms in about 60% of cases
B. Is an itchy skin disorder
C. Can be improved by a gluten free diet
D. Lesions can affect the scalp
E. Responds to steroids

Q3   Koebner's phenomenon is seen in:
A. Lichen planus
B. Viral warts
C. Psoriasis
D. Molluscum contagiosum
E. Queyrat's erythroplasia

Q4   Cutaneous manifestations of rheumatoid disease include:
A. Purpura
B. Pyoderma gangrenosum
C. Palmar erythema
D. Thickened skin due to excessive abnormal collagen
E. Pressure sores

Q5   Cutaneous manifestations of diabetes mellitus include:
A. Granuloma annulare
B. Erythema *ab igne*
C. Boils
D. Xanthomata on the buttocks
E. Erythema marginatum

Q6   Herpes zoster:
A. Mainly affects children
B. Causes severe pain which may precede the appearance of vesicular rash by 48 hours
C. Can be complicated by keratitis
D. Never involves the meninges
E. Only involves the sensory roots

Q7   Common warts:
A. Are caused by an RNA virus
B. Usually affect the trunk
C. Resistant cases can be treated by intralesional injection of bleomycin solution
D. Usually resolve spontaneously within two years
E. Can be treated by freezing with liquid nitrogen

Q8   The following favours a good prognosis in melanoma:
A. Male sex
B. A low Breslow thickness
C. Amelanosis
D. Involvement of the trunk
E. Regional lymphadenopathy

Q9   Albinos:
A. May have nystagmus
B. Lack the enzyme phenylalanine hydroxylase
C. Have a high incidence of squamous cell carcinoma
D. Have pale blond hair
E. Usually transmit the disorder in an autosomal dominant fashion

Q10   PUVA has the following side-effects:
A. An increased incidence of squamous cell carcinoma
B. Cataracts
C. Pruritus
D. Mycosis fungoides
E. Liver and marrow toxicity

Q11   The following are recognised causes of hirsutism:
A. Polycystic ovaries
B. Addison's disease
C. Turner's syndrome
D. Lichen planus
E. Congenital adrenal hyperplasia

Q12   Cutaneous manifestations of hypothyroidism include:
A. Hyperhidrosis
B. Diffuse hair loss
C. Pruritus
D. Fine hair
E. Pyoderma gangrenosum

Q13   The causes of penile ulcers include:
A. Lymphogranuloma venereum
B. Chancroid
C. Loiasis
D. Onchocerciasis
E. Granuloma inguinale

Q14   Topical corticosteroids are effective in:
A. Rosacea
B. Pityriasis versicolor
C. Cold sores
D. Athlete's foot
E. Molluscum contagiosum

Q15   Features of secondary syphilis include:
A. Tabes dorsalis
B. Condyloma latum
C. Snail-track ulcers
D. Gumma
E. Lymphadenopathy

Q16   Causes of finger clubbing include:
A. Bronchiectasis
B. Thyrotoxicosis
C. Iron deficiency
D. Psoriasis
E. Bacterial endocarditis

Q17   Pellagra is a recognised feature of:
A. Tryptophan therapy for depression
B. Carcinoid syndrome
C. High protein diets
D. Hartnup disease
E. Isoniazid therapy

Q18   Bullous pemphigoid:
A. Is more common in the Jewish race
B. Is treated with systemic steroids
C. May affect the oral cavity
D. Is characterised by intra-epidermal blisters
E. Presents with large tense blisters mainly on the back

Q19   The clinical features of Reiter's disease include:
A. Keratoderma blenorrhagica
B. Erosive arthritis
C. Lowe's syndrome
D. Low back pain
E. Circinate balanitis

Q20   Purpura is a feature of:
A. Cushing's syndrome
B. Thrombocytopenia
C. Wiskott-Aldrich syndrome
D. Menigococcal septicaemia
E. Vasculitis

Q21   Chicken pox:
A. Spreads by droplet infection from infectious patients
B. Can spread transplacentally
C. Is associated with Koplik's spots in the buccal mucosa
D. The rash consists of vesicles all of which appear simultaneously
E. Cannot be acquired by contact with cases of shingles

Q22   Indications for PUVA therapy include:
A. Mycosis fungoides
B. Resistant chronic pompholyx
C. Porphyria cutanea tarda
D. Psoriasis
E. Xeroderma pigmentosum

Q23   Hereditary angio-oedema:
A. Has an autosomal recessive inheritance
B. Is due to deficiency of the Clq part of the complement system
C. Can be fatal
D. Is a cause of urticaria
E. May present as an acute abdomen

Q24   Yellow discolouration of nails is a feature of:
A. Antimalarial therapy
B. Pustular psoriasis
C. Dermatophyte infections
D. Hypoalbuminaemia
E. Phenothiazine administration

Q25   The following are sexually transmitted:

A. Molluscum contagiosum
B. Vaginal candidiasis
C. Scabies
D. Rieter's disease
E. Forrestier's disease

Q26   The following skin lesions have a malignant potential:

A. Dermoid cyst
B. Cavernous haemangioma
C. Bowen's disease
D. Intradermal naevus
E. Erythroplasia of Queyrat

Section 11
Haematology

Q1 Sideroblastic anaemia may occur in:
A. Alcohol abuse
B. Lead poisoning
C. Myelodysplastic syndromes
D. Patients taking pyridoxine
E. Infectious mononucleosis

Q2 Glucose-6 phosphate dehydrogenase deficiency (G6PD)
A. Causes a defect in the Embden-Meyerhof pathway
B. Has an autosomal recessive inheritance
C. Can be precipitated by nitrofurantoin
D. Is a recognised cause of haemolytic anaemia
E. Can be precipitated by eating peas

Q3 In haemolytic anaemia:
A. The lifespan of a red cell is on average 150 days
B. There is likely to be bilirubin in the urine
C. If intravascular, there will be a reduced level of haptoglobins
D. Haemaglobinuria is a marker of severity
E. Mycoplasma infection is a recognised cause

Q4 The following features would suggest a primary rather than a secondary cause for a patient's poly- cythaemia:
A. Arterial oxygen saturation of 93%
B. Platelet count of 350×10^9/litre
C. Normal leukocyte alkaline phosphatase score
D. Splenomegaly
E. Normal red cell mass

60

Q5   Chronic idiopathic thrombocytopenic purpura in childhood:

A. Is defined as thrombocytopenia persisting beyond two months
B. Occurs in 2–5% of cases of acute ITP
C. Usually necessitates splenectomy
D. May be treated with anti-D immunoglobin
E. Is a feature of systemic-lupus erythematosus

Q6   Features of sickle cell disease in children include:

A. Nocturnal enuresis
B. Dactylitis
C. Haemosiderotic cardiomyopathy
D. Progressive splenomegaly
E. Salmonella osteomyelitis

Q7   With respect to cross-matching of blood for transfusion:

A. The patient's serum is screened for atypical IgM antibodies at 37°C using saline techniques
B. Direct Coomb's test is performed to detect antibodies in the patient against donor red blood cells
C. The erythrocytes from each donor unit are tested against the patient's serum at 37°C to detect IgG antibodies
D. The cross-match usually takes about 1 hour
E. If there is no time for cross-matching, group O–rhesus positive blood should be transfused.

Q8   The following laboratory results are compatible with a diagnosis of disseminated intravascular coagulation (DIC)

A. Prolonged thrombin time
B. Low platelet count
C. Elevated levels of fibrinogen degradation products in serum
D. Elevated fibrinogen levels in serum
E. Reduced factor VIII activity

Q9   Idiopathic thrombocytopenic purpura (ITP)
A. An auto-antibody can be demonstrated in about 70% of subjects
B. The auto-antibody cannot cross the placenta
C. The majority of cases respond temporarily to steroids (up to 3 mg/kg of prednisone)
D. When a patient with ITP is transfused with platelets, the transfused platelets survive longer than the patient's own platelets.
E. The intravenous administration of high dose IgG is a recognised treatment modality

Q10   The bleeding time may be prolonged in:
A. von Willebrand's disease
B. Vitamin K deficiency
C. Haemophilia A
D. Idiopathic thrombocytopenic purpura
E. Liver disease

Q11   Haemophilia A:
A. Causes a prolonged prothrombin time (PT)
B. Gene coding for the deficient factor is located on the long arm of the X-chromosome
C. Can be diagnosed prenatally by DNA analysis
D. Gene coding for the deficient factor has been cloned
E. Is characterised by low level of VIII:vWF

Q12   The partial thromboplastin time with kaolin (PTTK) is usually prolonged in:
A. Haemophilia A
B. von Willebrand's disease
C. Vitamin K deficiency
D. Idiopathic thrombocytopenic purpura
E. A patient who is fully heparanised

Q13   Recognised consequences of blood transfusion include:
A. Haemoglobinuria
B. Hypothermia
C. Hyperkalaemia
D. Air embolism
E. Amoebiasis

Q14 Multiple myeloma:
A. Is commoner in black people than in other racial groupings
B. When complicated by renal failure, responds poorly to high fluid intake
C. When complicated by hyperviscosity syndrome, may result in visual disturbance
D. Has a worse prognosis in patients with a higher serum B_2-microglobulin level at diagnosis
E. When treated with combination chemotherapy, has not been shown to be superior to intermittent melphalan in terms of survival.

Q15 With respect to Hodgkin's disease:
A. Lymphocyte predominant histology is associated with the best prognosis
B. The inguinal region is the commonest site for superficial lymphadenopathy at presentation
C. The presence of Reed–Sternberg cells is essential to making the diagnosis
D. The disease does not involve non-lymphatic tissue
E. Cyclical chemotherapy is the treatment of choice in patients with stage I disease

Q16 The following laboratory findings suggest iron deficiency anaemia:
A. Normal ferritin
B. Low serum iron
C. Complete absence of iron from macrophages in bone marrow
D. Low total iron binding capacity (TIBC)
E. Decreased mean corpuscular volume (MCV)

Q17 Considering vitamin K:
A. Fat malabsorption is the commonest cause of vitamin K deficiency in adults
B. None of the available preparations can be absorbed in the absence of bile salts
C. Vitamin dependent factors require the vitamin for carboxylation of their N-terminal residues so that they can chelate calcium
D. Vitamin K reverses warfarin effects almost instantaneously
E. Warfarin inhibits the reduction of 2,3-epoxide to quinone

Q18   With respect to erythropoiesis and erythropoietin:

A. Hypoxia is the main stimulus to erythropoietin production
B. Bilateral nephrectomy completely abolishes erythropoietin activity
C. Erythropoietin increases the maturation time of red blood cell precursors
D. Erythropoietin stimulates ALA synthetase activity in red blood cell precursors
E. Erythropoietin levels are found to be low in polycythaemia rubra vera (PRV)

Q19   Chronic lymphocytic leukaemia (CLL)

A. Frequently occurs in children
B. Is a T-cell leukaemia in most cases
C. May cause auto immune haemolytic anaemia
D. Should be treated once diagnosed
E. Median survival exceeds 50%

Q20   Acute lymphoblastic leukaemia (ALL)

A. Incidence peaks in middle childhood
B. Usually presents with lymphadenopathy
C. Associated with Philadelphia chromosome carries a good prognosis
D. Of the null-ALL immunological phenotype, has a good prognosis
E. Management should include craniospinal prophylaxis during remission

Q21   The typical laboratory findings in primary polycythaemia include:

A. High serum erythroprotein levels
B. Increased red cell mass
C. Initial thrombocytopenia
D. Neutropenia
E. Raised packed red cell volume

Q22   Recognised causes of familial thrombophilia include:

A. Homocystinuria
B. Factor V Leiden deficiency
C. Antiphospholipid syndrome
D. Behçet's syndrome
E. Protein C deficiency

Section 12
Medical Microbiology

Q1 *Klebsiella pneumoniae* **is**
A. A Gram-negative capsulate organism
B. A common cause of lobar pneumonia
C. Usually resistant to erythromycin
D. Sensitive to amoxycillin in approximately 50% of cases
E. Part of the commensal flora of the gastrointestinal tract

Q2 **Infections transmitted by unpasteurised milk include:**
A. Literiosis
B. Brucellosis
C. Q fever
D. Leptospirosis
E. Legionnaire's disease

Q3 **Falciparum malaria:**
A. Clinical features include haemoglobinuria
B. In early pregnancy, is best treated by mefloquine
C. May present one year after returning home from foreign travel
D. Is a recognised cause of convulsions
E. Is rarely complicated by thrombocytopenia

Q4 **Lyme disease:**
A. Is caused by *Coxiella burneti*
B. Is a tick-borne disease
C. May be diagnosed by using polymerase-chain reaction (PCR)
D. Is a recognised cause of myocarditis
E. Stage 1 is best treated with gentamicin

Q5   Regarding pseudomembranous colic:

A. It is a recognised side effect of clindamycin
B. It is caused by colonisation of the colon by *Clostridium perfringens*
C. Proctosigmoidoscopy is a useful investigation
D. The diagnosis may be made by demonstrating a positive Nagler reaction
E. The condition is effectively treated with aminoglycosides

Q6   The Mantoux test:

A. Involves injecting purified protein derivative (PPD) intramuscularly
b. Is positive in patients with tuberculosis
C. Becomes positive within 7 days of infection
D. Is more sensitive than the tine test
E. Involves CD34 cells

Q7   The identifying criteria of *Staphylococcus aureus* include:

A. Coagulase positivity
B. Phosphatase negativity
C. Fermentation of mannitol
D. Fluorescent greenish appearance of colonies
E. Serology by identification of Lancefield groups

Q8   The pathophysiological effects of endotoxins include:

A. Initial leucopenia
B. Release of interleukin I
C. Inhibition of Hageman factor
D. Activations of the alternative complement pathway
E. Stimulation of platelet aggregation

Q9   *Helicobacter pylori:*

A. Is a Gram-negative organism
B. Is associated with gastric carcinoma
C. Is frequently found in small intestinal mucosa
D. Activates complement
E. Is more likely to affect the gastric body than the antrum

Q10   *Haemophilus influenzae:*
A. Is a Gram-positive rod
B. Required X and V factors for growth
C. Causes influenza
D. Type b causes epiglottitis
E. Is a recognised cause of acute meningitis in primary school children

Section 13

Genetic Statistics and Molecular Biology

Q1   The following are more common in children with Down's syndrome:
A. Congenital hypothyroidism
B. Alopecia areata
C. Cutis marmorata
D. Imperfect canalisation of the nasolacrimal duct
E. Coeliac disease

Q2   The following are non-parametric statistical tests:
A. Wilcoxon's ran sum tests
B. Chi-squared
C. Student's
D. Mann-Whitney
E. Nemars

Q3   Which of the following statements related to the molecular basis of cystic fibrosis are true:
A. F508 is the most frequent genotypic mutation in northern European patients
B. The gene product is an exorcine cell membrane receptor
C. Pancreatic insufficiency is not related to the genotype
D. Ion transport regulation is defective
E. Mutation analysis may be accomplished by using the polymerase chain reaction

Q4   The sweat test:

A. May be falsely positive due to the use of flucloxacillin
B. May be falsely positive in Cushing's syndrome
C. Requires a total weight of sweat in excess of 100 mg
D. Reveals a chloride concentration in excess of sodium concentration in cystic fibrosis
E. Sum of sodium and chloride concentrations usually lies above 140 mmol/l in cystic fibrosis.

Q5   The following statements are correct:

A. In autosomal dominant inheritance, the abnormal gene may be situated on a sex chromosome
B. In autosomal dominant inheritance, the disease is always transmitted by an affected parent
C. In autosomal recessive inheritance, if two carrier parents marry there is a 25% chance of each child being affected
D. The genes coding for the human leukocyte antigen (HLA) are located on the long arm of chromosome 6
E. Grave's disease is associated with HLA types DR3 and B8

Q6   The polymerase chain reaction (*in vitro* enzymatic DNA amplification)

A. Can be used to amplify specimens several hundred years old
B. Can be used to diagnose muscular dystrophy
C. Can give false positive results even if the technique is correctly applied
D. Is a good diagnostic test for malaria
E. Requires a large specimen

Q7   Student's *t*-test:

A. Is a non-parametric statistical test
B. Distribution is normal at infinite degrees of freedom
C. Critical ratio is independent of the degrees of freedom
D. Is particularly useful for multivariant analysis
E. Can be used to study the effect of simvastatin or serum cholesterol levels

Q8   The standard deviation (SD)
A. Is the square root of the variance
B. Measures the spread of observations around the mean
C. Assesses the reliability of the mean
D. Can be manipulated mathematically
E. Is occasionally smaller than the standard error of the mean (SEM)

Q9   In a normal distribution:
A. The mean is lower than the mode
B. The mean equals the median
C. 95% of observations lie within the ISD of the mean
D. Student's *t*-test can be used
E. The coefficient of variation is unrelated to the SD

Q10   With reference to clinical trials:
A. In crossover designs, patients act as their own controls
B. The power of trial equals the type I error
C. Type I error describes the probability of false positives
D. Type 1 error describes the possibility of rejecting a null hypothesis when it is in fact valid
E. The number of patients required for the trial depends on type I and II errors

Q11   In screening for colorectal cancer, the haemoccult test:
A. Gives a cancer detection rate of 3/1000
B. Gives a rate of false positives of 5%
C. False positive results may be caused by carrots
D. Utilises a peroxidase enzyme to increase sensitivity
E. If positive, is an indication for colonoscopy

Q12   Audit:
A. Is derived from 'audition'
B. Demands confidentiality for success
C. Should focus only on patient outcome
D. Is a strategy for identifying and punishing wrongdoers
E. Is valuable in validating routine procedures

Q13 The following disorders are transmitted by autosomal dominant inheritance:

A. Phenylketonuria
B. Duchenne muscular dystrophy
C. Dubin–Johnson syndrome
D. Neurofibromatosis
E. Familial polyposis coli

Q14 The clinical features of Klinefelter's syndrome include:

A. XO genotype
B. Webbed neck
C. Small external genitals
D. Reduced libido
E. Coarctation of the aorta

Q15 A special diet plays an important role in the management of:

A. von Gierke's disease
B. von Willebrand's disease
C. Wilson's disease
D. Phenylketonuria
E. Marfan's syndrome

Q16 The inheritance of the following disorders is X-linked:

A. Marfan's syndrome
B. Haemophilia A
C. Cystic fibrosis
D. Huntingdon's chorea
E. Hunter's syndrome

Q17 With reference to genetics:

A. Exons are the non-coding sequences of genes
B. Proto-oncogenes code for protein involved in signal transduction between cell membranes and nucleus
C. Anti-oncogenes are tumour suppressant genes
D. DNA polymerase is the enzyme used by retroviruses to construct DNA
E. Polymerase chain reaction (PCR) refers to the technique of DNA amplification by biologic replication in a host cell

Q18 **In a study investigating telomerase activity in breast cancer, 7 out of 10 node-positive invasive cancers and 0 out of 8 node-negative cancers had detectable telomerase activity These groups could be compared using:**
A. The standard chi-squared test
B. McNemar's test
C. The two sample t-test
D. Fisher's exact test
E. The chi-squared test with Yate's continuity correction

Q19 **When analysing the differences in paired samples, the following types of data and appropriate methods of analysis are crossed paired:**
A. Ordinal data – sign test
B. Nominal data – Stuart test
C. Dichotomous data – McNemar's test
D. Interval data with large samples (> 100) – Wilcoxon matched pairs test
E. Interval data with small samples and non-normal distribution – paired t-test

Q20 **When comparing two samples, the following types of data and appropriate statistical methods are correctly paired:**
A. Interval data with large samples – chi-squared for trend
B. Interval data with small samples, normal distribution and uniform variance – two sample t-test
C. Dichotomous data with large samples and expected frequencies > 5 – Fisher's exact test
D. Dichotomous data with small samples and expected frequencies < 5 – chi-squared test with Yate's correction
E. Interval data with small samples and non-normal distribution – Mann–Whitney W test

Q21 **The paired t-test is:**
A. Impractical for samples < 50
B. Based on a negatively skewed distribution
C. Useful for the analysis of quantitative data
D. Used for two independent samples
E. Not applicable to samples larger than 100

Q22   In a chi-squared test for a 3 × 2 contingency table:
A. There are two degrees of freedom
B. At least three cells must have expected values greater than 5
C. All the observed values must be greater than 1
D. An expected frequency can be zero
E. Variables must be quantitative

Q23   Fisher's exact test for a contingency table:
A. Is suitable when the expected frequencies are small
B. Usually gives a smaller probability than the ordinary chi-squared test
C. Is more difficult to calculate when the expected frequencies are small
D. Is a parametric test
E. Is equivalent to the chi-squared test with Yate's continuity correction

Section 14
Thermoregulation

Q1   Hypothermia:
A. Is determined as a core body temperature below 32°C
B. Is characterised by shivering
C. May be caused by benzodiazepines
D. Is due to hypothyroidism in 30% of cases
E. Causes a delta wave on the ECG

Q2   Recognised causes of hyperthermia include:
A. Salicylates poisoning
B. Spinal cord injury
C. Seizures
D. Barbiturates
E. Exercise

Q3   The clinical features of hypothermia include:
A. Diuresis
B. Metabolic acidosis
C. Clinical improvement with dantrolene therapy
D. Acute pancreatitis
E. Polycythaemia rubra vera

Q4   The ECG changes of hypothermia include:
A. Delta wave
B. Ventricular fibrillation
C. Prolonged PR interval
D. Prolonged QT interval
E. J wave

Answers to
Multiple-choice Questions

Oncology

A1:   A(T)   B(T)   C(T)   D(F)   E(F)
The commonest type of ionising radiation used in clinical practice is x-rays which are produced artificially by linear accelerators. The severity of DNA damage is oxygen dependent, hypoxic cells are more resistant to radiotherapy than well-oxygenated cells. Grays (Gy) describe the energy absorbed per unit mass. Cancer patients are treated by external beam, interstitial or intracavity radiotherapy. The effects of radiotherapy depend on the dose, the tumour size, the tumour proliferation rate, the tumour radiosensitivity and the presence of anaemia and vascular disease. Radiotherapy can be palliative or curative. It can be given pre, intra or post operatively.

In sarcoma management, radiotherapy is indicated for positive margins, high grade tumours and recurrent disease.

A2:   A(F)   B(F)   C(T)   D(F)   E(F)
RNA and protein synthesis occurs during the resting phase G1. Duplication of cellular DNA occurs during the S phase and a second resting phase (G2) follows which precedes mitosis (M). The duration of the cell cycle varies from 20 to 110 hours. The rate of tumour growth decreases exponentially with time (Gompertzian pattern) therefore the growth fraction of small tumours is greater than that of larger ones. Cytotoxic drugs usually act on cycling cells and can be phase or non-phase specific.

A3:   A(F)   B(F)   C(T)   D(F)   E(F)
EBV is a member of the herpes family and is associated with Burkitt's lymphomas and nasopharyngeal carcinoma. There are around 50 types of HPV. The virus is associated with anal and cervical cancer. HBV is associated with hepatocellular carcinoma, however the mechanism of oncogenesis remains unclear. HTLV-1 is the only known RNA virus which causes a human malignancy.

A4:   A(F)   B(F)   C(F)   D(T)   E(F)
The risk factors include late menopause, postmenopausal obesity (premenopausal obesity is protective), early menarche, nulliparity, later first pregnancy, combined oral contraceptives, hormone replacement therapy, family history of breast cancer, high intake of animal fat, high alcohol consumption and ionising radiation.

A5:   A(F)   B(F)   C(T)   D(T)   E(T)
Screening mammography has reduced breast cancer mortality by 30% in women over the age of 50 years. 20% of screen-detected cancers are ductal carcinomas *in situ* (DCIS). Premenopausal obesity is a protective factor whereas obesity after the menopause tends to increase the risk. Familial breast cancer (FBC) accounts for approximately 5% of cases. The typical features of FBC include bilaterality, early presentation (before the age of 45 years) and the involvement of a first degree relative. Several genes are responsible for FBC, these include BRCA-1, BRCA-2, p53, ataxia telangiectasia and androgen receptor gene.

A6:   A(T)   B(F)   C(T)   D(F)   E(F)
Secondary bone neoplasms are far commoner than primary neoplasms. Primary tumours that commonly metastasise to bone include prostatic adenocarcinoma, thyroid cancer, invasive breast cancer, pulmonary carcinoma and renal adenocarcinoma. Ductal carcinoma in situ rarely metastasise as the proliferating epithelial cells are confined to the ductal system without breaching the basement membrane.

A7:   A(F)   B(F)   C(T)   D(T)   E(T)
Progestins are used in the treatment of endometrial carcinoma whereas oestrogens can cause and promote this malignancy. The endocrine therapies used in the management of breast cancer include tamoxifen (an oestrogen antagonist), aromatase inhibitors such as formestane and arimidix, GHRH-analogues, progestins and aminoglutathimide.

A8:   A(T)   B(T)   C(F)   D(T)   E(F)
E-cadherins are transmembrane glycoproteins which mediate haemophilic adhesions between cells. Down regulation of E-cadherins is associated with dedifferentiation and metastasis of cells. There are at least eight members of metalloproteinases which are responsible for degrading the extracellular matrix. Scatter factor secreted by fibroblasts stimulates the motility of tumour cells. Tumour cells adhere to the endothelial cells

via integrins, selectins and CD44 molecules.

A9: A(T) B(T) C(F) D(T) E(F)

Cisplatinum and cyclophosphamide are effective in the treatment of ovarian cancer. Several cytotoxic drugs are used in the treatment of testicular teratoma. These include bleomycin, etoposide and cisplatinum. Anal SCC is primarily treated by radiotherapy and chemotherapy (5-fluouracil and mitomycin C).

A10: A(T) B(F) C(F) D(F) E(T)

Carcinoid tumours arise from APUD cells and secrete serotonin. The incidence is 1.5 per 10^5 per year and 45% of lesions arise in the appendix. 24-hourly urine 5-HIAA is used in diagnosis. The carcinoid syndrome (flushing, bronchospasm and colicky abdominal pain) is found in 9% of cases. The tumours are associated with right-sided cardiac abnormalities such as tricuspid stenosis. Surgical excision is the mainstay of management. 35% of tumours respond to chemotherapy.

A11: A(T) B(F) C(T) D(T) E(F)

Oncogenes have been isolated from approximately 15% of human cancers. Growth suppressor genes are anti-oncogenes.

A12: A(F) B(F) C(T) D(T) E(T)

The enlargement of an organ in hyperplasia results from an increase in the number of its specialised constituent cells. The persistence of growth following the withdrawal of the stimulus is a feature of neoplasia and not hyperplasia.

Section 2
Clinical Pharmacology

A1:   A(F)   B(F)   C(F)   D(T)   E(F)

Atenolol is a water-soluble cardioselective beta-blocker with less effects on β_2-receptors. It is associated with coldness of the extremities and impaired glucose tolerance test. It is effective in the treatment of hypertension and reduces the recurrence rate of MI.

A2:   A(T)   B(T)   C(F)   D(F)   E(F)

ACE inhibitors have a valuable role in all grades of heart failure. They are also used in the immediate and long term management of patients who have had an MI. The reduction in serum aldosterone due to ACE inhibitors may cause hyperkalaemia and therefore caution should be exercised when using these drugs concomitantly with potassium-sparing diuretics. ACE inhibitors reduce or abolish glomerular filtration and are likely to cause severe and progressive renal failure. They are thus contraindicated in patients known to have renovascular disease. Renal function and electrolytes should be checked before starting ACE inhibitors and monitored using treatment.

A3:   A(F)   B(F)   C(T)   D(T)   E(T)

Enoxaparin (Clexane) is a low molecular weight heparin (LMWH) that is as effective and as safe as conventional unfractional heparin. It is used in DVT prevention and treatment. Heparin is a recognised cause of immune mediated thrombocytopenia which usually occurs after 6–10 days of use. This complication is less likely with LMWH.

A4:   A(T)   B(F)   C(T)   D(T)   E(F)

Biphosphonates are absorbed onto hydroxyapatile crystals thus reducing the rate of growth and dissolution. The rate of bone turnover associated with disease is reduced by biphosphates. The indications for biphosphates include ostelytic lesions and bone pain associated with breast cancer or multiple myeloma, Paget's disease of bone, hypercalcaemia of malignancy

80

and postmenopausal osteoporosis. They should be used with caution in patients with renal impairment, cardiac disease and epilepsy. Pamidronate is only available in an infusion form whereas clodronate is available as an oral preparation.

A5:   A(T)   B(T)   C(T)   D(F)   E(F)
Drugs with antimuscarinic activity dilate the pupil and paralyse the ciliary muscle. Pilocarpine and carbachol stimulate the muscarinic receptors and are therefore miotics and have parasympathomimetic side effects such as sweating, bradycardia and intestinal colic.

A6:   A(F)   B(F)   C(F)   D(F)   E(F)
Chronic simple glaucoma is due to obstruction of trabecular meshwork. These drugs are recognised treatment modality for the condition. Dorzolamide is a topical carbonic anhydrase inhibitor. 'Latanprost' is a prostaglandin analogue which increases the uveoscleral outflow of aqueous humour.

A7:   A(F)   B(T)   C(F)   D(F)   E(F)
Warfarin as an anticoagulant becomes effective 72 hours after the first dose. This is because the clotting factors already present in the circulation need to be eliminated. The half life of this drug is 36 hours and it is terminated mainly by hepatic metabolism. Cimetidine inhibits the enzyme system that metabolises warfarin thus prolonging its duration of action.

A8:   A(T)   B(F)   C(T)   D(F)   E(T)
Frusemide is a loop diuretic that inhibits active chloride and sodium reabsorption in zones II and III of the nephron. It also increases the urinary secretion of calcium and magnesium. It is more effective than thiazides in patients with a low GFR. It tends to reduce urinary excretion of gentamicin thus increasing the risk of ototoxicity and nephrotoxicity.

A9:   A(F)   B(T)   C(F)   D(T)   E(F)
Most insulin-dependent diabetics require 40 units of insulin per day. The crystalline form of insulin zinc suspension is a long-acting insulin with activity lasting 30–36 hours. Insulin requirements in diabetics increases in systemic illness such as septicaemia, trauma and surgery.

A10:   A(T)   B(T)   C(F)   D(T)   E(T)
Metformin does not seem to rely on beta cells for its action therefore it

reduces blood glucose in pancreatectomised animals. Chlorpropamide has an anti-diuretic (ADH-like) effect that causes water retention and dilutional hyponatraemia thus exacerbating cardiac failure. The drug is excreted unchanged in urine and it is not therefore recommended in patients with renal failure. Tolbutamide has a shorter duration of action than chlorpropamide and is mainly metabolised in the liver.

A11: A(T) B(T) C(F) D(T) E(T)

Metronidazole inhibits alcohol and aldehyde dehydrogenase causing a disulfiram-like action. It is particularly effective against anaerobic micro-organisms when one of its metabolics binds to DNA, thus impairing nucleic acids synthesis. Large doses of metronidazole have been shown to be carcinogenic in rodents, but no study has shown carcinogenicity in humans.

A12: A(F) B(F) C(F) D(T) E(T)

Carbimazole metabolite methimazole is usually concentrated in the thyroid glands within minutes of administration. Carbimazole renders thyrotoxic patients euthyroid in 4–8 weeks of therapy. It can be given to children at an initial dose of 15 mg daily. The adverse effects include pruritus, arthralgia, sore throat (leucopenia), nausea, headaches and rarely alopecia. Caution should be exercised when the drug is given to pregnant or breast feeding women.

A13: A(T) B(T) C(F) D(F) E(T)

NSAIDs vary in the selectivity for inhibiting different types of cyclo-oxygenases (COX). Selective inhibition of COX-2 is claimed to improve gastrointestinal tolerance. NSAIDs commonly damage intestinal and gastric mucosa by inhibiting the synthesis of certain prostaglandins that reduce gastric acid secretion and exert cytoprotective effect. These drugs are therefore contraindicated in patients with peptic ulceration. The inhibition of renal prostaglandins leads to sodium and water retention thus antagonising the antihypertensive effects of beta blockers. The inhibition of thromboxane synthesis in platelets makes these drugs effective in reducing mortality due to cardiovascular disease. There has been a recent interest in their potential role in cancer prevention.

A14: A(T) B(T) C(F) D(F) E(F)

Morphine stimulates the chemoreceptor trigger zone causing nausea and vomiting. Histamine release may cause pruritus. The third cranial nerve nucleus is inhibited by morphine and meiosis ensues. Morphine also stimulates ADH release, increases the tone in the intestinal wall and inhibits peristalsis. The latter two effects cause constipation.

A15: A(T) B(F) C(T) D(T) E(T)
Tamoxifen is an anti-oestrogen with partial agonist activity. It has been shown to prolong survival and reduce local recurrence in women with estrogen receptor-positive (ER-positive) tumours regardless of age. ER-negative tumours also respond but the response rate is relatively low (10% vs. 60%). The incidence of DVT and endometrial carcinoma is slightly increased in women taking tamoxifen. (1 per 1000 per year). Tamoxifen has beneficial effects on bone and cardiovascular system in post menopausal women.

A16: A(T) B(F) C(T) D(T) E(F)
Omeprazole has a long duration of action (> 12 h). It is effective in the treatment of gastric ulcers (20 mg daily for 8 weeks), duodenal ulcers (20 mg daily for 4 weeks) and erosive reflux oesophagitis (20–40 mg for 4–8 weeks). Omeprazole inhibits hepatic microsomal enzymes and can delay the elimination of phenytoin, warfarin and diazepam.

A17: A(T) B(T) C(F) D(F) E(T)
Teicoplanin, transexamic acid and fluconazole are eliminated mainly by renal mechanisms and renal impairment lead to accumulation of such drugs. Serum creatinine and creatinine clearance can guide the dosage. Simvastatin is contraindicated in patients with acute liver failure.

A18: A(F) B(F) C(F) D(T) E(T)
The amount of thiazides, valproate and paracetamol excreted in breast milk are too small to be harmful. Ciprofloxacin should be avoided in breast feeding women due to high concentrations in breast milk. Cimetidine is excreted in large amounts but is not known to be harmful.

A19: A(F) B(T) C(T) D(T) E(T)
Sulphonylureas are associated with increased risk of hypoglycaemia in severe liver disease and can produce jaundice. Suxamethonium can cause prolonged apnoea in patients with hepatic impairment due to reduced hepatic synthesis of pseudocholinesterase. Rifampicin should be avoided or used is small doses (< 8 mg/kg) in hepatic impairment due to risk of hepatotoxicity.

A20:   A(F)   B(F)   C(F)   D(F)   E(F)
Phenytoin seems to accelerate metabolism of the above drugs thus reducing their effect.

A21:   A(T)   B(F)   C(F)   D(F)   E(T)
L-Dopa is usually combined with a dopa-carboxylase inhibitor such as benserazide and carbidopa that inhibit the peripheral degradation of L-Dopa to dopamine. L-Dopa improves bradykinesia and rigidity more than tremor. Closed-angle glaucoma is a contraindication to the use of the drug.

A22:   A(T)   B(T)   C(F)   D(F)   E(T)
Penicillamine is a disease-modifying antirheumatic drug that acts by stabilising lyosomes in white blood cells. It is also used in copper and lead poisoning. Stevens-Johnson and Goodpasture's syndromes are recognised complications. Other complications include anorexia, fever, leucopenia, proteinuria, anaemia, thrombocytopenia and rashes.

A23:   A(T)   B(T)   C(F)   D(T)   E(T)
Full blood count and serum biochemistry should be monitored regularly.

A24:   A(T)   B(F)   C(T)   D(F)   E(T)
80% of 5-fluorouracil is metabolised by the liver and only 20% of the drug is excreted unchanged in urine. It is an antimetabolite that inhibits the formation of essential nucleic acids thus interfering with DNA/RNA synthesis and causing cell death. It is commonly used in the treatment of colorectal carcinoma (stage C and liver metastasis). Mesna is given in conjunction with cyclophosphamide and ifosfamide in order to reduce urinary bladder toxicity.

A25:   A(F)   B(T)   C(T)   D(F)   E(F)
Cephradine and cephazolin are first generation cephalosporins which have generally been replaced by newer generations that are less susceptible to degradation by penicillinases. Cefuroxime is a second generation drug. Third generation drugs include cefotaxime, ceftazidime, cefodizime and ceftriaxone. These drugs are more active than cefuroxime against Gram-negative bacteria. It has good penetration into the CSF, therefore it is of value in the treatment of meningitis.

A26:   A(T)   B(T)   C(F)   D(F)   E(F)

Ranitidine reduces gastric acid secretion by blocking H2 receptors. It is excreted mainly unchanged by the kidneys and dose accumulation due to renal failure can lead to confusion. Omeprazole is the drug of choice in the treatment of erosive reflux oesophagitis (grade IV). Cimetidine is a recognised cause of gynaecomastia due to blockage of androgen receptors.

A27: A(T) B(T) C(F) D(F) E(F)
Acyclovir is active against herpes viruses but does not eradicate them. It is selectively toxic due to the greater affinity of viral thymidine kinase and viral DNA polymerase. High oral doses are required for severe shingles. Zidovudine inhibits reverse transcriptase and is effective against HIV infection.

A28: A(F) B(F) C(T) D(T) E(F)
Antiepileptic drugs control seizures by enhancing GABA-mediated inhibition (benzodiazepines, vigabatrim, phenobarbitone and valproate) or a reduction in Na^+ flux (phenytoin, carbamazepine, valproate and Lamotrigine). Vigabatrin is an irreversible inhibitor of GABA-T which converts GABA into succinic semialdehyde. The increased availability of GABA in the brain mediate the action of many antiepileptic drugs.

A29: A(F) B(T) C(F) D(T) E(T)
Amoxycillin inhibits bacterial wall synthesis. It is inactivated by penicillinase-producing bacteria. It has an ability to diffuse through the outer phospholipid membrane of Gram-negative bacteria which makes it effective against 50% of *E. coli* and 85% of *H. influenzae* strains.

A30: A(F) B(T) C(T) D(F) E(T)
Statins act by inhibiting HMG CoA reductase activity. Cholecystyramine and colestipol are anion exchange resins which increase the excretion of bile acids causing more cholesterol to be converted to bile acids. Gemfibrozil and bezafibrate produce a modest decrease in LDL and increase in HDL and a marked decrease in triglycerides. The latter seems to result from stimulation of lipoprotein lipase activity.

A31: A(F) B(F) C(F) D(T) E(T)
Ciprofloxacin and trimethoprim work by inhibiting bacterial nucleic acid synthesis. Ciprofloxacin inhibits DNA gyrase and trimethoprim inhibits dihydrofolate reductase. Gentamicin works by inhibiting bacterial protein

synthesis. Penicillins, cephalosporins and vancomycin inhibit cell wall synthesis.

A32: A(F) B(T) C(T) D(F) E(T)
Lignocaine is a class IB agent that blocks the voltage dependent Na^+ channels and is therefore effective in treating ventricular dysrhythmias. Adenosine stimulates Adenosine A_1-receptors and open K^+-channels thus stowing conduction in the AV-mode. Verapamil is a class IV agent that inhibits Ca^{2+} influx.

A33: A(T) B(T) C(F) D(F) E(F)
Muscarinic effects also include pupillary constriction, bronchial constriction, hypotension (due to bradycardia and vasodilatation), an increase in gastrointestinal motility and secretion, contraction of urinary bladder and sweating. The nicotinic effects of acetylcholine include stimulation of autonomic ganglia (tachycardia and vasoconstriction), however these effects are weaker than the muscarinic effects.

A34: A(T) B(T) C(F) D(T) E(T)
Losartan is a new drug that reduces the blood pressure by blocking angiotensin-1 receptors. Amlodipine is a calcium-channel blocker. Quinidine is effective in the treatment of supraventricular and ventricular arrhythmias but has anticholinergic effects. Milrinone inhibits phosphodiesterase III causing a rise in intracellular cAMP and in Ca^{2+} influx. It increases myocardial contractility and vasodilatation. Minoxidil is a potent vasodilator that causes severe fluid retention.

A35: A(F) B(T) C(F) D(F) E(T)
Effects of sympathetic stimulation include pupillary dilatation, increased glycogenolysis, increased glucogenesis, vasoconstriction in the skin, vasodilatation in skeletal muscle and relaxation of gastrointestinal tract and urinary bladder.

A36: A(T) B(T) C(F) D(T) E(F)
The interaction with ergostrerol forms pores through which essential fungal cell constituents are lost. It is poorly absorbed orally and is therefore given intravenously or intrathecally. It is effective against *Aspergillus* sp, *Candida* sp and *Cryptococcus* sp. The drug is nephrotoxic and should be discontinued if renal damage occurs.

A37: **A(T)** **B(F)** **C(T)** **D(T)** **E(T)**

Acetylcysteine is another antidote for paracetamol poisoning. Desferri-oxamine is the antidote for iron poisoning. Flumazenil is the antidote for benzodiazepine overdose. Carbon monoxide from car exhausts is probably the commonest cause of serious self-poisoning especially in men.

A38: **A(F)** **B(T)** **C(T)** **D(F)** **E(T)**

Cyterabine inhibits DNA polymerase and methotrexate inhibits dihydrofolate reductase. Doxorubicin is an antibiotic that intercalates between base pairs. Alkylating agents such as mustine, cyclophos-phamide, chlorambucil, busulphan and cisplatin form covalent cross-links. Some of these drugs are cycle specific, e.g. cytarabine (S-phase-specific) and vinca alkaloids (M-phase specific).

A39: **A(F)** **B(F)** **C(T)** **D(T)** **E(T)**

Pyoderma gangrenosum is a recognised feature of inflammatory bowel disease and is treated by corticosteroids. Hypokalaemia may ensue due to minoralocorticoid effects. Other adverse effects of corticosteroids include peptic ulceration, adrenal suppression, psychosis, diabetes, growth suppression in children, osteoporosis, hypertension and immunosuppression. The latter effect is due to depression of monocyte and macrophage function and depletion of CD4 cells.

A40: **A(F)** **B(T)** **C(F)** **D(T)** **E(F)**

Aspirin is a weak acid that acts by inhibiting the cyclo-oxygenase (COX) enzyme which converts phospholipids into prostaglandins. Most patients will not tolerate the adverse effects (nausea, vomiting, epigastric pain and tennitus) caused by the high doses of soluble aspirin necessary to achieve an anti-inflammatory effects. The propionic acid derivatives such as ibuprofen have fewer side effects and are tried first in patients with inflammatory arthropathy. Aspirin has been recently shown to reduce the incidence of colorectal and breast cancer probably by inhibiting the COX type II enzyme.

Section 3
Cardiology

A1: A(T) B(T) C(F) D(F) E(T)
The sympathetic outflow to the failing heart increases in order to increase heart rate and myocardial contractility. Cardiac failure decreases renal perfusion which in turn stimulates the renin–angiotensin–aldosterone system. The Starling curve is shifted in a downward direction in cardiac failure.

A2: A(T) B(T) C(F) D(T) E(F)
Mitral valve prolapse prevalence rates are 4–17% in women and 2–12% in men. Prevalence falls with increasing age in women, but remains static in men. Most people have no symptoms but 60% of people have non-specific symptoms and the condition (mitral valve prolapse syndrome) is associated with chest pain. Infective endocarditis occurs in 2–8% of patients with mitral valve prolapse and post mortems have shown thrombi on mitral valve leaflets in patients who had died of cerebral emboli. The commonest indication for mitral valve replacement in elderly people is myxomatous degeneration and mitral valve prolapse.

A3: A(F) B(T) C(T) D(T) E(F)
Conduction delay tends to make the sound of valve closure (i.e. S1) quieter and the converse is also true. Pericardial effusions make every-thing quiet.

A4: A(F) B(T) C(F) D(F) E(T)
Renin converts angiotensin (α_2-globulin) into angiotensin I. The latter is converted into angiotensin II by converting enzymes. Angiotensin II increases aldosterone secretion, decreases renin output and increases vascular tone. Aminopeptidase converts angiotensin II into angiotensin III. The latter is degraded by angiotensinases.

A5: A(F) B(F) C(F) D(T) E(F)
Balloon valvuloplasty is more likely to be successful in the long term if

the valve cusps are pliable and not heavily calcified. The combination of hydralazine and isosorbide dinitrate has been shown to reduce mortality compared with placebo. Metolazone is a thiazide-like diuretic. Long term digoxin therapy has been shown to improve symptoms and exercise tolerance in patients in sinus rhythm but its effect on survival is unknown.

A6:   A(T)   B(F)   C(T)   D(F)   E(T)
Carotid chemoreceptors may be stimulated by hypoxia resulting in vasoconstriction and tachycardia (increased blood pressure). The aortic and carotid chemoreceptors are stretch receptors, the discharge of which decreases with the sudden assumption of the upright posture. The latter increases sympathetic output to the peripheral vascular system causing vasoconstriction.

A7:   A(F)   B(F)   C(F)   D(F)   E(F)
Poor predictors of outcome include a previously housebound lifestyle, cancer, renal failure and pneumonia, but not age. About 14% of survivors are discharged from hospital. If a monitor is not available, a 200 J d.c. shock should be applied, as VF is the most treatable rhythm. Recent studies have shown that endotracheal adrenaline is not adequately absorbed. Famous cases exist of children being resuscitated after falling into frozen lakes after long periods but the discharge rate for patients brought to A&E with no pulse was 1 in 211 in a recent study.

A8:   A(F)   B(F)   C(T)   D(F)   E(T)
Hypokalaemia causes ST depression and T-wave inversion and prolonged QT intervals.

A9:   A(T)   B(F)   C(F)   D(T)   E(T)
The aortic knuckle 'X' is produced by the aortic arch, 'Y' represents the superior vena cava. 'Z' is part of the right atrium.

A10:   A(F)   B(F)   C(F)   D(T)   E(T)
Systemic hypertension, thyrotoxicosis and hypothermia usually result in increased cardiac output.

A11:   A(T)   B(F)   C(T)   D(F)   E(T)
The internal jugular vein represents a continuation of the sigmoid sinus at the jugular foramen. It runs alongside the chain of deep cervical lymph nodes. It lies lateral to the internal carotid artery within the carotid

sheath. The vein passes anterior to the thoracic duct on the left side.

A12:   A(T)   B(T)   C(F)   D(T)   E(F)

The angiographic appearance of the atrial appendage helps to distinguish between the left and right atrium. There are some anastomoses between the two coronary arteries, e.g. Vieussen's ring, the Lugel's artery and between the anterior and posterior descending arteries. It should be noted that these anastomoses may not be sufficient to prevent infarction once an artery has been occluded. The sinus node artery arises from the right coronary artery in 55% of cases. The circumflex artery gives rise to this artery in the remaining cases.

A13:   A(T)   B(F)   C(T)   D(T)   E(F)

The 'a' wave is due to atrial systole. It is therefore prominent in tricuspid stenosis and in conditions that increase the right ventricular and diastolic filling pressure (RVDFP). It is absent in atrial fibrillation (AF). Cannon 'a' waves are seen in complete heart block where the right atrium (RA) contracts against a closed tricuspid valve. E is incorrect because the aortic valve (AV) is on the left side of the heart.

A14:   A(F)   B(T)   C(F)   D(T)   E(T)

There are three types of dissection in the Debakey classification. Type I involves the ascending and descending aorta. Type II is confined to the ascending aorta, and type III is confined to the descending aorta. Type III dissections are best treated medically initially. MRI scanning has been found to be a useful technique to evaluate a suspected aortic dissection but availability is a problem. Transoesophageal echocardiography has the additional advantage of being able to show the ostia and proximal coronary arteries.

A15:   A(T)   B(F)   C(F)   D(T)   E(T)

AF may be precipitated by acute hypovolaemia. Lone AF is associated with a low risk of stroke. Beta blockers are the drugs of choice in the treatment of AF secondary to thyrotoxicosis provided cardiac failure is not a problem. Independent clinical predictors of an increased risk of stroke in subjects with non-rheumatic AF are:

- Recent (within three months) onset of CCF
- History of hypertension
- History of previous TIA or CVA

A14: A(T) B(F) C(F) D(T) E(T)
The heart's conduction system changes with age. Fifty per cent of the sinus node in the young adult comprises pacemaker cells, decreasing to less than 10% after the age of 75. More than half of the left bundle branch may be replaced by fibrous tissue from the sixth decade. No specific age related changes have been identified in the AV node or His bundle. In a series of 89 patients of 80 years or older, 50% of them had an improvement in dizziness or congestive cardiac failure after the insertion of a pacemaker. Pacemakers are sometimes required as a back-up when anticoagulants or anti-tachycardia drugs are needed by the patient.

A17: A(F) B(T) C(T) D(F) E(F)
Echocardiographic features of HOCM are: the ratio of the septal to posterior left ventricle wall of at least 1:3, the M-mode features of the left ventricle outflow tract, the systolic anterior motion of the mitral valve and the premature systolic closure of the aortic valve. The most important predictor of sudden death is the presence of non-sustained ventricular tachycardia on holster monitoring. Amiodarone improves survival; class 1 anti-arrhythmics and B-blockers do not prevent sudden death.

A18: A(F) B(T) C(T) D(F) E(T)
CHD occurs in 1% of live births. The aetiology of CHD involves maternal rubella infection, maternal alcohol abuse, and genetic and hormonal abnormalities. The clinical features include central cyanosis, pulmonary hypertension, growth retardation, heart failure, syncope, paradoxical embolism, finger clubbing and squatting. The last mentioned refers to the posture adopted by children with Fallot's tetralogy. This posture reduces venous return and thus improves cerebral oxygenation.

A19: A(T) B(T) C(T) D(F) E(T)
The usual ECG axis at birth is +135°. Left axis deviation is associated with tricuspid atresia, ventricular septal defects and endocardial cushion defects. The T wave inverts after three days in leads V4 and V1. The inverted T waves in leads V2 and V3 become upright after five years of age. PR interval elongation occurs with atrioventricular septal defects. Ebstein's anomaly, myotonic dystrophy and cardiomyopathy. Short PR intervals occur in Wolff–Parkinson–White, Lown–Ganong–Levine syndromes, Duchenne muscular dystrophy, Pompe's disease and hypertrophic obstructive cardiomyopathy.

A20:   A(T)   B(F)   C(F)   D(F)   E(T)
Renin release is inhibited by β-blockers, hyperkalaemia and angiotensin
II. The latter inhibits renin release through a negative feedback mech-
anism.

A21:   A(F)   B(F)   C(F)   D(T)   E(F)
The third heart sound is diastolic in timing and occurs just after the
second heart sound. It is due to rapid ventricular filling as soon as the
mitral and tricuspid valves open. It is normal in children and young
adults. However, it may be associated with cardiac failure in subjects over
the age of 40 years. It is a low-pitched sound which is best heard with the
diaphragm of the stethoscope.

A22:   A(T)   B(F)   C(F)   D(F)   E(F)
The consequences of assuming the upright position include venous pool-
ing in capacitance vessels, reduced cardiac output, increased total
peripheral resistance, decreased cerebral blood flow ($\downarrow PO_2$, $\downarrow PCO_2$),
tachycardia and stimulation of the renin–angiotensin–aldosterone system.

Section 4
Respiratory Medicine

A1: **A(T)** **B(T)** **C(T)** **D(T)** **E(T)**
Amiodarone and sulphasalazine cause interstitial lung disease, nebulised pentamidine is linked with pneumothorax, aspirin can cause bronchospasm and the contraceptive pill predisposes to pulmonary embolus.

A2: **A(F)** **B(T)** **C(F)** **D(F)** **E(T)**
Legionnaire's disease is notifiable in Northern Ireland and Scotland but not in England and Wales. Infections are monitored by voluntary reporting to the Communicable Disease Surveillance Centre. Most cases occur in people between the ages of 40 and 70 years with males affected three times more commonly than females. Most cases are sporadic with less than 25% occurring in outbreaks. Pontiac fever is also caused by Legionella organism but no fatalities have been recorded.

A3: **A(F)** **B(F)** **C(T)** **D(T)** **E(F)**
As the name implies, obstructive sleep apnoea (OSA) is due to frequent (> 10/h) episodes of pharyngeal collapse to which a variety of factors predispose. It occurs in children and can lead to systemic and pulmonary hypertension, and IHD. Acetazolamide causes a metabolic acidosis and is therefore sometimes useful in central sleep apnoea but not OSA.

A4: **A(F)** **B(F)** **C(F)** **D(T)** **E(F)**
TB is a notifiable disease though there is significant under reporting. Three negative smears are required to be considered not infectious. It is recommended that patients be isolated for the first two weeks of treatment only. AAFB are often visible in the sputum after this, but they are non-viable. Only about 5% of patients with AIDS in England and Wales develop TB.

A5: **A(F)** **B(F)** **C(F)** **D(T)** **E(F)**
The transverse thoracis muscle lies deep to the internal intercostal muscle. The intercostal neurovascular structures pass in the subcostal groove

behind the inferior border of the rib. This fact should be borne in mind when performing thoracostomy for pneumothorax or pleural effusion. The anterior intercostal arteries of the upper five spaces arise from the internal thoracic arteries.

A6:   A(F)   B(T)   C(T)   D(F)   E(F)
The respiratory neurons are located in the medulla. H^+ ions of metabolic acidosis increase ventilation mainly by stimulating peripheral chemo-receptors such as the carotid bodies. These positively charged ions penetrate the blood–brain barrier very poorly and therefore have a limited effect on central chemoreceptors. The apneustic centre lies in the caudal part of the pons, whereas the pneumotaxic centre lies in the upper part of the pons. The pontine centres modify the activity of the medullary centres.

A7:   A(T)   B(T)   C(F)   D(F)   E(T)
Acute upper airway obstruction causes respiratory acidosis characterised by a raised blood pH. Bradycardia is a late and dangerous sign. Poly-cythaemia is a recognised feature of chronic obstructive airways disease.

A8:   A(T)   B(T)   C(F)   D(F)   E(T)
Polycythaemia and decreased concentration of 2,3-DPG inside the red cell shift the curve to the left.

A9:   A(F)   B(F)   C(T)   D(F)   E(T)
Streptococcal pneumonia accounts for 60–75% of community acquired pneumonias compared with Mycoplasma pneumonia (5–18%). There is a 21-fold increase in the risk of death or need for ITU when two or more of the following are present:

1. Diastolic BP < 60 mmHg
2. Respiratory rate > 30/min
3. Serum urea > 7 mmol/l

A10:   A(F)   B(F)   C(F)   D(F)   E(T)
The main cells implicated in the inflammatory response are the eosinophil and the mast cells. Exacerbations are episodic and lung function usually

returns to normal afterwards. Spirometry shows an obstructive defect with reduced expiratory flow with traditionally a 15% variability. Mortality is increasing. Frequent use of a β-agonist is a marker of disease severity and should be acted upon.

A11:   A(F)   B(T)   C(F)   D(F)   E(F)

Histology showing organising buds of connective tissue within the alveolar ducts is required to make the diagnosis, though BAL is recommended to exclude infection. Although steroids are generally effective, a negative response does not exclude the diagnosis.

A12:   A(T)   B(T)   C(F)   D(T)   E(T)

Laryngotracheobronchitis is the commonest cause of acute stridor in paediatrics. It is usually distinguishable from acute epiglottitis due to *Haemophilus influenzae* type b by the presence of a viral prodrome, barking cough and harsh stridor. Dysphagia, drooling and toxic appearance usually accompany acute epiglottitis. Pharyngeal oedema due to infectious mononucleosis may cause acute stridor which is treated with steroid therapy. C1 esterase inhibitor deficiency causes recurrent acute stridor with angiodema. Inheritance is usually autosomal dominant. Fresh frozen plasma is required in the acute management. Laryngomalacia (floppy larynx syndrome) causes chronic stridor.

A13:   A(F)   B(F)   C(T)   D(T)   E(T)

Chronic lung disease is defined as oxygen dependence beyond four weeks of age and has a multifactorial aetiology including: barotrauma, oxygen toxicity, pulmonary oedema and infection. 15–45% of infants under 1500 g ventilated for hyaline membrane disease develop chronic lung disease. Dexamethasone is of benefit in ventilator dependence. Diuretics improve lung mechanics, theophylines augment diuretics and act as a respiratory stimulant. Prevention is by reducing pre-term delivery, length of ventilation and reduction in ventilator pressure.

A14:   A(T)   B(T)   C(T)   D(F)   E(T)

Trichitillomania refers to hair loss secondary to hair being broken from self-induced trauma.

A15:   A(T)   B(F)   C(F)   D(F)   E(F)

Skin involvement and anterior uveitis occur in 10% and 25% of cases, respectively. Hypercalcaemia complicates 10% of cases. The fatality rate in American blacks is about 8% compared with 4% in U.K. subjects.

A16: A(T)   B(F)   C(F)   D(T)   E(T)
Respiratory acidosis is characterised by a high PCO_2 and low blood pH. Renal compensation tends to increase serum bicarbonate in order to correct the acidosis.

A17: A(T)   B(T)   C(T)   D(T)   E(F)
Asbestosis fibres cause pulmonary fibrosis and restrictive pulmonary disease. The fibres may remain in the lung for decades, therefore disease progression can occur without further asbestos exposure. Pulmonary fibrosis may result in finger clubbing, reduced CO transfer factor and cor pulmonale. Other consequences of asbestos exposure include malignant pleural mesothelioma, benign pleural disease and increased risk of bronchial carcinoma.

A18: A(F)   B(F)   C(T)   D(T)   E(F)
ARDS is characterised by non-carcinogenic pulmonary oedema. PCWP measurements helps to distinguish the condition from pulmonary oedema due to left ventricular failure. ARDS reduces pulmonary compliance. Corticosteroids have no important role in management.

A19: A(T)   B(F)   C(F)   D(T)   E(T)
Goodpasture's syndrome is caused by an anti-basement membrane antibody, affects the glomeruli and lungs and may cause haemoptysis. Hypertrophic pulmonary osteoarthropathy occurs in approximately 3% of cases, particularly squamous cell carcinomas and adenocarcinomas. Other non-metastatic manifestations include anorexia, hypercalcaemia, hypo-glycaemia, thyrotoxicosis, SIADH secretion, encephalopathy, myopathy (Eaton–Lambert syndrome), thrombophlebitis migrans, anaemia, DIC, finger clubbing (30%), dermatomyositis and herpes zoster.

A20: A(T)   B(T)   C(F)   D(F)   E(F)
Type 1 respiratory failure is caused by diseases that interfere with gas exchange by damaging lung tissue. Hypoxaemia results from right to left shunt and/or ventilation-perfusion mismatch. The initial compensatory increase in total ventilation renders PCO_2 normal or low. Patients tend to breathe rapidly with a low tidal volume.

A21:   A(T)   B(T)   C(F)   D(F)   E(F)
The diagnosis of ARDS is based on identifying a precipitating cause (i.e. sepsis, trauma, pancreatitis, etc), refractory hypoxaemia ($PO_2 < 8\,kPa$, $FiO_2 > 0.4$), radiological evidence of bilateral diffuse pulmonary infiltrates, a pulmonary artery occlusion pressure (PAOP) < 15–$18\,mmHg$ and a reduced total lung compliance ($< 30\,ml/cmH_2O$).

Section 5
Gastroenterology

A1:   A(F)   B(F)   C(T)   D(F)   E(F)

Acute pancreatitis is idiopathic in 10–30% of cases. It may be a side effect of sodium valproate therapy. When secondary to alcohol, it has an overall majority of about 5% compared with 10–25% for gallstone associated and idiopathic pancreatitis. Chronic pancreatitis is associated with pancreatic cancer, especially the tropical and hereditary forms of the disease.

A2:   A(F)   B(F)   C(T)   D(T)   E(F)

Irritable bowel syndrome occurs more frequently in women than men. Those with diarrhoea predominantly have short colonic transit times, and those with constipation predominating have long transit times. Balloon distension of the rectum produces symptoms in 50–60% of patients compared with less than 10% of controls.

A3:   A(T)   B(T)   C(F)   D(T)   E(F)

The azygos tributaries anastomose with the tributaries of the left gastric vein which drains into the portal vein (portal systemic anastomosis). The oesophagus lies posterior to the left recurrent laryngeal nerve. About 50% of carcinomas occur in the middle third and the remainder are equally divided between the other two thirds.

A4:   A(T)   B(F)   C(T)   D(T)   E(F)

Postsystemic anastmoses are seen at the lower end of the oesophagus, between the superior rectal veins (portal) and the middle and inferior rectal veins (systemic), and between the diaphragmatic veins (systemic) and liver veins.

A5:   A(T)   B(F)   C(F)   D(F)   E(T)

VIP inhibits gastric acid secretion and inhibits small intestinal reabsorption. Excessive levels of VIP (e.g. 3000 pg/ml) result in watery diarrhoea syndrome (WDHA syndrome). Extrapancreatic tumours account for 10% of WDHA syndrome.

A6: A(T) B(F) C(F) D(T) E(F)
300 mg of bilirubin is equivalent to 6 g of haemoglobin. β-Glucoronidase enzymes deconjugate bilirubin in the intestine. Conjugated bilirubin is secreted against a concentration gradient; therefore an active transport system is required. Urobilinogens are colourless whereas urobilins are coloured.

A7: A(F) B(T) C(T) D(T) E(F)
Advanced liver damage in PBC as assessed by histology may not correlate with the clinical and biochemical changes. PBC may be associated with a number of other autoimmune disorders including Sjögren's syndrome, scleroderma, rheumatoid arthritis and fibrosing alveolitis. Ursodeoxycholic acid has been shown to improve both symptomatic and biochemical features of the disease. PBC can recur after liver transplantation.

A8: A(F) B(F) C(T) D(T) E(F)
Few facts are always true in medicine but UC does always involve the rectum. Peak age is 20–40. Fibrosing alveolitis is a recognised association of both UC and sulphasalazine therapy. Sulphasalazine causes reversible oligospermia and should be avoided in men wishing to start a family, but it is thought to be safe in pregnancy.

A9: A(T) B(T) C(F) D(T) E(F)
Biliary output of cholesterol is increased and synthesis of bile acid is reduced by oestrogen therapy. Gallstones are commoner in women than men across all age groups. About 80% of patients with gallbladder cancer have gallstones with a particularly high risk in those with longstanding stones or stones greater than 3 cm in diameter. Only radiolucent cholesterol stones can be dissolved with solvents such as methyl-*tert*-butyl ether.

A10: A(F) B(T) C(F) D(T) E(F)
The histopathological appearances of coeliac disease on jejunal biopsy include subtotal villous atrophy and crypt elongation/hyperplasia. Increased villous cell loss is accompanied by a compensatory increase in crypt cell replication. The columnar epithelial cells become pseudostratified or cuboidal. There is an increase in plasma cells in the lamina propria with a concomitant decrease in lymphocytes. Epithelioid granulomata occur in Crohn's disease.

A11:   A(F)   B(F)   C(T)   D(T)   E(F)
Histamine stimulates gastric acid secretion. H_1-blockers do not effect gastric acid secretion whereas H_2-blockers suppress acid secretion.

A12:   A(F)   B(F)   C(T)   D(F)   E(T)
The daily bile secretion into the duodenum is approximately 500 ml. Cholesterol solubility decreases as the relative molar concentration increases. CCK-PZ contracts the gallbladder and relaxes the sphincter of Oddi. Most bile acids are reabsorbed in the terminal ileum.

A13:   A(T)   B(T)   C(F)   D(T)   E(T)
The sequence of the five amino acids at the C-terminal of gastrin is identical to that of CCK-PZ. Secretin stimulates pancreatic electrolyte secretion. Antimuscarinic agents reduce pancreatic secretion. It also causes gall bladder contraction. VIP is similar in structure to secretin.

A14:   A(F)   B(T)   C(T)   D(T)   E(T)
Noradrenaline decreases intestinal secretion. Prostaglandins are thought to contribute to the diarrhoea caused by inflammatory bowel disease and radiation enteritis.

A15:   A(T)   B(T)   C(F)   D(T)   E(F)
Chlyomicrons pass into the lacteal vessels (lymph). Medium-chain triglycerides (MCTs) are more water-soluble than long-chain triglycerides.

A16:   A(T)   B(F)   C(F)   D(T)   E(T)
PT may be increased owing to vitamin K deficiency.

A17:   A(F)   B(F)   C(F)   D(T)   E(T)
Crypt abscesses are more conspicuous in ulcerative colitis. Pseudopolyps are a feature of ulcerative colitis. Carcinoma is a less frequent complication in Crohn's disease.

A18:   A(F)   B(F)   C(F)   D(T)   E(F)
Cholesterol gallstones are usually solitary, averaging 1.5 cm in diameter, and pale brown in colour. Diabetes mellitus is associated with increased cholesterol concentration. Cholesterol stones may be visible on plain x-rays as a shell of calcium deposited on the surface of the stone. Bile pigment stones may complicate chronic haemolytic anaemias.

A19: A(T) B(T) C(T) E(F) E(T)

Hypergammaglobulinaemia may develop in liver failure as less antigen is removed from the portal blood by the diseased liver. Ammonia may play an important part in causing encephalopathy. Factor VIII is synthesised by the vascular endothelium.

A20: A(T) B(T) C(T) D(T) E(T)

A, B, C and D are examples of opportunistic infections.

A21: A(T) B(F) C(F) D(T) E(F)

M represents the coeliac axis arising from the aorta. It gives rise to the splenic artery 'O'. 'P' is the spleen. The coeliac axis usually arises at the level of the thoraco-lumbar junction, and therefore this cut lies higher than L2.

A22: A(T) B(F) C(T) D(F) E(T)

Hypercalcaemia is a recognised cause of pancreatitis. Excessive alcohol intake is the commonest aetiological factor. Budd–Chiari syndrome causes post-hepatic portal hypertension (hepatic vein thrombosis).

A23: A(T) B(T) C(F) D(F) E(T)

Vitamin B_{12} deficiency may lead to spinal cord degneration and megaloblastic anaemia. The incidence of gallstones is increased in bile acid deficiency. Diarrhoea may be due to fat malabsorption and bile-induced colitis.

A24: A(F) B(T) C(T) D(T) E(T)

All these tests detect pancreatic enzymes whereas the pentagastrin test measures gastric acid after stimulation.

A25: A(F) B(T) C(T) D(T) E(T)

Direct urease testing is the first line procedure whens endoscopy is being performed. Serology yields equivalent results and is useful in epidemiology. Urea breath tests are also helpful and are mainly used to demonstrate eradication after therapy.

A26:   A(F)   B(T)   C(T)   D(F)   E(F)
Video and fibre optic gastroscopy yields equivalent results and are more reliable than barium meal examination overall. Procedures maybe conducted without sedation and this is often safer. Complications and deaths often relate to cardio-respiratory problems in the elderly.

A27:   A(T)   B(F)   C(T)   D(T)   E(F)
Mallory-Weiss tears are usually self limiting. No anti-acid therapy has been proved to be effective in in-patients.

A28:   A(F)   B(F)   C(T)   D(T)   E(T)
Hypoglycaemia and hypokalaemia are common consequences of FHF. Asteraxis is a sign of encephalopathy. Other consequences of FHF include coagulopathy, thrombocytopenia, respiratory alkalosis, ARDS, acute renal failure, sepsis, cardiac failure, reduced total peripheral resistance, gastro-intestinal haemorrhage, encephalopathy and cerebral oedema.

Section 6
Neurology

A1: A(T) B(F) C(F) D(T) E(F)
The EMG shows no visible changes in the electrical action potential when the muscle is relaxed.

A2: A(F) B(T) C(T) D(T) E(F)
During hyperpolarisation, the potassium channels are more active than the sodium channels. In myelinated axons, ionic exchange occurs mainly at the nodes of Ranvier and this means that less metabolic energy is required in such fibres to pump the ions out once the impulse has passed. Myelination also increases the conduction velocity. Saltatory conduction (Latin *saltare* – to leap) is a feature of myelinated fibres where the active region leaps from one node to another.

A3: A(T) B(F) C(T) D(T) E(F):
Calcaneovalgus is the opposite to equinovarus and is a feature of tibial nerve palsy. In equinovarus the foot is plantar-flexed and inverted.

A4: A(F) B(T) C(T) D(F) E(T)
Interruption of the parasympathetic fibres supplying the constrictor pupillae results in pupil dilatation. Ptosis results from paralysis of levator palpebrae superioris. The afferent pathway of the consensual light reflex consists of the optic nerve, optic chiasma and optic tract and the efferent pathway consists of the opposite oculomotor nerve which is intact.

A5: A(F) B(T) C(T) D(F) E(T)
The detrusor muscle is innervated by parasympathetic nerves (S3–S4) and the external sphincter is innervated by spinal nerves (S2–S3).

A6: A(F) B(F) C(T) D(T) E(F)
Foot drop and paraesthesia of the lateral aspect of the foot are features of common peroneal nerve palsy. Failure of knee extension results from paralysis of quadriceps femoris. The thigh adductors are supplied by the obturator nerve.

A7:   A(T)   B(T)   C(F)   D(F)   E(T)
Hypoxia and hypercapnia increase cerebral bood flow, whereas autonomic mechanisms seem to be unimportant.

A8:   A(T)   B(F)   C(T)   D(T)   E(F)
The medial cord branches includes the:

1. Medial head of the median nerve
2. Ulnar nerve
3. Medial pectoral nerve
4. Medial cutaneous nerve of the arm
5. the medial cutaneous nerve of the forearm
6. The pronator teres is supplied by the lateral head of the median nerve

A9:   A(F)   B(T)   C(F)   D(T)   E(F)
The facial nerve gives off the chorda tympani approximately 5 mm above the stylomastoid foramen. The mandibular branch passes just behind the angle of the mandible. The mastoid antrum and air cells lie posterior to the facial nerve.

A10:   A(T)   B(F)   C(F)   D(F)   E(T)
Golgi tendon organs are part of the inverse myotactic reflex. The afferents of the stretch reflex are Type Ia fibres (70–120 m/s) that have a large diameter. Disynaptic inhibitory synapses onto the antagonistic motor neurons are part of the stretch reflex.

A11:   A(T)   B(F)   C(T)   D(T)   E(F)
The BBB allows transport of substances in both directions and its endothelial cells have six times the mitochondria found in endothelial cells elsewhere in the body.

A12:   A(F)   B(F)   C(F)   D(T)   E(F)
Normal CSF contains monocytes (5/mm^3) but no polymorphs. The presence of oligoclonal bands signifies a diagnosis such as multiple sclerosis. The protein concentration in the normal CSF is approximately 300 mg/l and immunoglobulins constitute 15% of total protein. The CSF blood glucose concentration exceeds 50% of that of the plasma and a low level of glucose is a feature of bacterial meningitis.

A13:   A(F)   B(T)   C(F)   D(F)   E(T)
There is a negative potential of the inside (in) of the axon relative to the outside (out). The cell membrane is permeable to sodium, potassium and chloride and the internal potential is related to the concentrations of ions through the Goldman equation:

$$V_M = 58 \log \frac{P_K[K^+_{out}] + P_{Na}[Na^+_{out}] + P_{Cl}[Cl^-_{out}]}{P_K[K^+_{in}] + P_{Na}[Na^+_{in}] + P_{Cl}[Cl^-_{in}]}$$

A14:   A(F)   B(T)   C(F)   D(T)   E(F)
The synaptic potential channels are ligand-gated. The postsynaptic potential is excitatory when depolarising and is inhibitory when GABA binds to postsynaptic receptors.

A15:   A(T)   B(F)   C(F)   D(T)   E(F)
Sodium channels open within less than one millisecond and remain open for a maximum of a few milliseconds. The channels are most dense in the nodes of Ranvier ($12\,000/\mu m^2$). Tetrodotoxin is a recognised blocking agent to sodium channels.

A16:   A(T)   B(F)   C(F)   D(T)   E(T)
Ataxia and dysarthria are features of vertebrobasilar system insufficiency. Amaurosis fugax refers to the sudden loss of vision in either eye due to transient emboli in the retinal arteries.

A17:   A(T)   B(F)   C(F)   D(T)   E(F)
Two point discrimination, joint position and vibration sensations travel through the posterior column.

A18:   A(F)   B(T)   C(F)   D(T)   E(F)
The sole of the foot is innervated by S1 root and the groin is innervated by L1. The index finger corresponds to C7.

A19:   A(F)   B(F)   C(F)   D(T)   E(F)
The posterior cerebral artery arises from the basilar artery and the posterior inferior cerebellar artery arises from the vertebral artery. The middle cerebral artery supplies the lateral surface of each cerebral hemisphere. The inferior petrosal sinus drains into the internal jugular vein.

A20:   **A(T)**   **B(F)**   **C(F)**   **D(F)**   **E(F)**

The median nerve gives off no branches in the arm. It supplies the first two (lateral) lumbricals and innervates the palmar aspect of the lateral 3½ fingers. The ulnar half of the flexor digitorum profundus is supplied by the ulnar nerve and the dorsal aspects of the lateral 2½ fingers are innervated by the radial nerve.

A21:   **A(T)**   **B(F)**   **C(T)**   **D(T)**   **E(T)**

The biceps muscle is innervated by the muculocutaneous nerve.

A22:   **A(T)**   **B(F)**   **C(F)**   **D(F)**   **E(F)**

The neurons described in B, C, D and E statements are cholinergic.

A23:   **A(T)**   **B(F)**   **C(T)**   **D(F)**   **E(F)**

Cholinergic stimulation results in detrusor muscle contraction, gall bladder contraction and penile erection. Ejaculation is mediated by the parasympathetic system.

A24:   **A(T)**   **B(T)**   **C(F)**   **D(F)**   **E(T)**

Drugs with cholinergic activity such as pilocarpine, carbachol and anticholinesterases (e.g. neostigmine) are miotics.

A25:   **A(T)**   **B(T)**   **C(F)**   **D(F)**   **E(T)**

The lateral two lumbricals and the abductor pollicis brevis are supplied by the median nerve.

A26:   **A(F)**   **B(F)**   **C(F)**   **D(F)**   **E(T)**

CSF is contained in the subarachnoid space. The spinal segment T12 lies at the level of the 9th thoracic vertebra. The spinothalamic tracts transmit pain and temperature and the posterior column transmits light touch, two-point discrimination and vibration sensations. Hemisection of the spinal cord results in ipsilateral paralysis and contralateral loss of pain and temperature below the level of the section.

A27:   **A(F)**   **B(F)**   **C(F)**   **D(T)**   **E(F)**

S1 root innervates the lateral aspect of the foot (sensory), plantar flexors of the foot and the ankle jerk.

A28: A(F) B(F) C(T) D(T) E(F)
Following the initial presentation, SAH has a 50% of recurrence in the first month. Six months after presentation, the annual risk of rebleeding is approximately 3%.

A29: A(T) B(T) C(T) D(T) E(T)
Neurological complications occur eventually in about 70% of HIV infected patients with clinical illness. They may be the presenting features of the disease in 15% of patients.

A30: A(T) B(F) C(F) D(F) E(T)
The gait of Parkinson's disease is shuffling. Lesions of the cerebellar vermis result in ataxic gait. The abnormal gait of polyneuropathy may be bilateral.

A31: A(F) B(T) C(F) D(T) E(F)
Limb-girdle dystrophy is recessively inherited whereas Becker's and Duchenne's muscular dystrophies are X-linked.

A32: A(T) B(T) C(F) D(T) E(F)
Tabes dorsalis, Friedreich's ataxia and SCDC may affect the posterior column of the cord that transmits vibration, position and two-point discrimination sensory modalities.

A33: A(T) B(T) C(F) D(T) E(T)
Benign intracranial hypertension is associated with young obese females rather than young slim males.

A34: A(T) B(T) C(F) D(F) E(F)
Farber's lipogranulomatosis is due to ceramidase deficiency. The adult type Gaucher's disease is due to glucocerebrosidase and metachromatic leukodystrophy is linked to arylsulphatase A deficiency.

A35: A(T) B(T) C(T) D(T) E(T)
Ipsilateral hemiplegia and sixth nerve palsy can occur as false localising signs in association with intracranial space-occupying lesions.

A36: A(T) B(F) C(F) D(T) E(F)
Primary delusions represent a first rank symptom in schizophrenia and memory is usually intact in this condition.

A37:   A(F)   B(F)   C(T)   D(F)   E(F):
Clouding of consciousness and memory disturbances are features of organic disorders. Secondary and not primary delusions are a recognised feature of depressive illness. Grandiose delusions occur in mania and visual hallucinations are seen in schizophrenia and organic mental disorders, including substance abuse.

A38:   A(T)   B(T)   C(T)   D(F)   E(F)
Memory disturbance is a feature of organic disorders and somatic passivity is seen in schizophrenia.

A39:   A(T)   B(F)   C(T)   D(T)   E(T)
Farber's disease is a storage disorder due to defective ceramidase.

A40:   A(F)   B(T)   C(T)   D(T)   E(F)
Cocaine addiction accounts for approximately 10% of new notifications for drug misuse in the UK. The clinical features include depression, psychosis, paranoia and violent behaviour. Fluoxetine may reduce cocaine craving.

Section 7
Endocrinology

A1: A(T) B(F) C(F) D(T) E(T)

Glucocorticoids are secreted episodically with a pronounced diurnal variation. The peak occurs in the early morning and then occurs around midnight. Glucocorticoids have mineralo-corticoid effects, stimulate gluconeogenesis, inhibit the immune system, and inhibit collagen synthesis and catabolic effects on muscle.

A2: A(T) B(F) C(T) D(F) E(T)

ADH is secreted by the posterior pituitary gland. Secretion is stimulated by increased osmolarity, stress stimuli and hypoglycaemia. Causes of inappropriate ADH secretion include pulmonary disease, congestive cardiac failure and small cell bronchial carcinoma.

A3: A(F) B(T) C(T) D(T) E(F)

Prolactin is a 199 aminoacid hormone secreted by chromophobe cells of the anterior pituitary gland. Causes of excess secretion include pregnancy, prolactinomas (micro or macro), primary hypothyroidism, pituitary stalk damage, chest wall injuries, adrenal insufficiency, Cushing's syndrome and drugs including oestrogens, metoclopramide, methyldopa, opiates and reserpine. Bromocriptine and dopamine have inhibitory effects on prolactin secretion.

A4: A(F) B(F) C(F) D(T) E(T)

Vasopressin (ADH) is synthesised in the supraoptic nucleus of the hypothalamus and transported to the posterior pituitary via axoplasmic flow. ADH deficiency leads to diabetes insipidus which is characterised by polyuria and thirst. ADH excessive secretion impairs the ability to excrete a water load and may lead to water intoxication.

A5:   A(F)   B(F)   C(T)   D(T)   E(T)

Growth hormone (GH) is synthesised by somatotropes which are a subclass of the pituitary (anterior) acidophilic cells. It is secreted episodically in response to hypothalamic GHRH with much of the secretion occurring at night. Secretion is stimulated by hypocalcaemia and amino acids such as arginine. GH acts principally on the liver where it controls the secretion of insulin-like growth factor-I (IGF-I) which in turn acts on cartilage and soft tissues.

A6:   A(F)   B(F)   C(T)   D(F)   E(T)

Insulin reduces lipolysis in adipose tissue and ketogenesis in the liver. It increases glycogen synthesis glucose uptake by tissues and protein synthesis (anabolic effect)

A7:   A(T)   B(F)   C(T)   D(F)   E(F)

TSH is secreted by basophil cells in the anterior pituitary gland. The half-life of T4 is 6–7 days, therefore it cannot be administered more than once daily. The maximal activity of T4 is not reached until 7–10 days after administration compared with 24 hours for T3 which is more valuable in the emergency treatment of myxoedema coma.

A8:   A(F)   B(T)   C(T)   D(T)   E(F)

Glucocorticoids have minelaro-corticoid effects causing water and sodium retention and potassium excretion. Glucocorticoids induce lipocortins which inhibit phospholipase A2 thus decreasing the production of prostaglandins and leucotrienes.

A9:   A(T)   B(T)   C(F)   D(T)   E(F)

ADH causes peripheral vasoconstriction and has a direct negative inotropic effect on the heart. The effects of ADH also include stimulation of ACTH secretion and increased release of factor VIII and von Willebrand's factor thus contributing to haemostasis.

A10:   A(F)   B(T)   C(T)   D(T)   E(F)

LHRH secretion by the hypothalamus is pulsatile. It controls the release of FSH and LH by the anterior pituitary. The LH response is greater during the luteal phase. LHRH analogues such as goserelin and buserelin down regulate the pituitary receptors to decrease the secretion of FSH and LH. These drugs are used in the treatment of breast cancer in premenopausal women and prostatic cancer in men.

A11: A(F) B(T) C(F) D(T) E(F)

Testosterone decreases scalp hair but increases body hair. The hormone stimulates protein synthesis (anabolic effect) and inhibits LH secretion by the pituitary gland. Testosterone patches can be used to treat patients with primary testicular failure.

A12: A(T) B(T) C(T) D(F) E(F)

Other clinical features of Cushing's syndrome include central obesity, hypertension, osteoporosis, striae, depression peptic ulceration, reduced libido, acne and poor wound healing. The causes of the syndrome include pituitary hyperplasia, pituitary adenoma, ectopic ACTH-secreting tumours, adrenal tumours, adrenal gland hyperplasia and glucocorticoid therapy.

A13: A(F) B(T) C(T) D(F) E(T)

The clinical features of Addison's disease include postural hypotension, hypo-glycaemia, lethargy, depression, abdominal pain, vomiting, fever, tachycardia and increased skin pigmentation. The latter is due to excessive ACTH and melanocyte-stimulating peptides. The disease may be associated with other auto immune disorders such as vitiligo, pernicious anaemia and myxoedema.

A14: A(T) B(F) C(F) D(F) E(F)

A 21-hydroxylase deficiency is due to a mutation of a gene located on chromosome 5. The mutation affects 1 in 40 live births and approximately 1 in 7400 births develop the clinical disorder. The clinical features include water and salt depletion, virilisation, hirsutism, sexual precocity with pseudo puberty (in males) and amenorrhoea. The lack of aldosterone may lead to hyperkalaemia. The various clinical features are due to deficiency of aldosterone and cortisol and excess of androgens. Treatment is by mineralocorticoid and glucocorticoid replacement as for Addison's disease. The condition is 5 times more common than 11-hydroxylase deficiency.

A15: A(F) B(T) C(F) D(T) E(F)

Grave's disease is an autoimmune disorder caused by antibodies to the TSH receptors causing stimulation and excess T4 and T3 production. The disease usually presents during the third and fourth decades. Serum TSH is usually low with increased levels of T4, T3 and autoantibodies. Treatment modal-ities include anti-thyroid drugs (carbimazole, methimazole and propylthio-uracil) β-blockers, radioactive iodine and subtotal thyroidectomy. The latter is considered if the medical treatment fails or the goitre causes com-pression symptoms.

Section 8
Nephrology

A1: A(F) B(T) C(T) D(F) E(T)
The ascending loop of Henle is impermeable. Under normal physiological conditions, very little protein is excreted in urine (< 150 mg/day). The action of ADH on the distal tubule produces a concentrated urine. The Na^+ and K^+/H^+ exchange in the distal tubule is controlled by aldosterone and not ADH.

A2: A(T) B(T) C(T) D(F) E(F)
Hyperkalaemia and tertiary hyperparathyroidism are recognised features of CRF.

A3: A(F) B(F) C(F) D(T) E(F)
Microalbuminuria is defined are urinary excretion of albumin that is persistently elevated above normal which is not detectable by conventional semiquantitative test strips. It is only deemed present after infection and structural abnormalities of the urinary tract have been excluded. It predicts mortality from cardiovascular disease in diabetic and elderly subjects. Most insulin-dependent diabetic patients with microalbuminuria have retinopathy, but usually this is of the background variety. In microalbuminuric patients, strict metabolic control by continuous subcutaneous insulin infusion has been effective in reducing the albumin excretion rate. Persistent elevation in albumin excretion rates is exceptional in the first five years of insulin-dependent diabetes.

A4: A(T) B(T) C(F) D(F) E(T)
Total cholesterol triglycerides LDL and VLDL cholesterol are typically raised in the nephrotic syndrome whilst HDL is reduced. These changes occur because of an increase in hepatic cholesterol and lipoproteins and an increase in urinary excretion of HDL. Diabetic nephropathy is the commonest cause of nephrotic syndrome and end-stage renal failure in

the United States. Protein loading has been shown to increase urinary protein exchange and worsen hypoalbuminaemia. Hypercoagulability is a recognised complication of the nephrotic syndrome.

A5:   A(F)   B(T)   C(T)   D(F)   E(T)

It is exceptional for nephropathy to develop within 10 years of IDDM. Predictors include microalbuminuria, hyperfiltration and rising blood pressure. Diabetics in ESRF have an increased mortality because of coronary and cerebral vascular disease. Progression can be slowed but not stopped by treatment of BP.

A6:   A(F)   B(T)   C(T)   D(F)   E(F)

A7:   A(F)   B(F)   C(T)   D(F)   E(F)

Isotope renography will, at best, detect 90% of renal artery stenoses. There is a high prevalence of atherosclerotic renal artery stenosis in the elderly population and up to 40% of these subjects will have renal impairment. Diuretics are thought not to be helpful in the treatment of renovascular hypertension because blood pressure is inversely related to the total exchangeable sodium concentration.

A8:   A(T)   B(F)   C(F)   D(F)   E(T)

β-Blockers, hyperkalaemia and angiotensin inhibit renin release.

A9:   A(T)   B(F)   C(F)   D(T)   E(T)

A10:   A(T)   B(T)   C(T)   D(T)   E(F)

Hyperventilation, alkalinisation with sodium bicarbonate and administration of insulin/dextrose will shift potassium into the intracellular compartment. β_2-Adrenoreceptor agonists will promote intracellular uptake of potassium by AMP-dependent activation of the Na^+/K^+ pump. Sodium or calcium exchange resins can be given orally and rectally. Their action starts within 30 minutes and lasts for 6 hours.

Section 9

Rheumatology and Immunology

A1:   A(T)   B(F)   C(F)   D(T)   E(T)

Class II HLAs are controlled by the D region. Matching at the B and DR loci has a greater influence on graft survival than matching at A, B and C loci. ABO blood group compatibility is essential for all transplants.

A2:   A(T)   B(T)   C(F)   D(T)   E(F)

The onset of gout before the age of 30 in men and in any premenopausal woman should raise the question of a specific enzyme defect leading to marked purine overproduction or an inherited defect in renal tubular handling. Allopurinol is a xanthene oxidase inhibitor and is the drug of choice for long-term therapy. The adverse effects of allopurinol include rashes, vasculitis, hepatitis, interstitial nephritics and toxic epidermal necrolysis. Serum uric acid is neither sufficiently sensitive nor specific enough to be used as a diagnostic test.

A3:   A(F)   B(F)   C(T)   D(T)   E(T)

Behçet's disease is an illness of the second to fourth decade. Renal impairment is uncommon but when it occurs, it is often due to amyloidosis. Vasculitis of the coronary arteries may lead to myocardial infarction. Thalidomide is effective in the treatment of severe recurrent aphthous stomatitis, Cyclosporin is more effective in the treatment of ocular problems and mucocutaneous lesions.

A4:   A(F)   B(T)   C(F)   D(T)   E(F)

Dermatomyositis (DM) and polymyositis (PM) are the most commonly acquired myopathies (excluding toxins) in developing countries. Diagnosis requires a compatible clinical picture, raised creatinine kinase activity, EMG changes and muscle biopsy showing necrosis and inflammation. DM produces a more acute onset of symptoms and is characterised by capillary damage on muscle biopsy. PM has a more insidious onset with no capillary damage. Arthralgia is common in DM but rare in PM, only usually seen when there is associated interstitial lung disease.

A5: A(F) B(T) C(T) D(T) E(F)
Factors predisposing to osteoporosis and bone fractures include female sex, oestrogen lack, excessive alcohol consumption, Cushing's syndrome, immobility and heparin.

A6: A(T) B(T) C(T) D(T) E(T)
Bisphosphonates are potent inhibitors of bone resorption. The dose of etridonate needed to inhibit bone resorption also impairs mineralisation of newly synthesised bone matrix. Other bisphosphonates such as pamidronate inhibit resorption at concentrations which are much lower than that which impairs mineralisation. Side-effects of sodium fluoride include gastric irritation and a lower extremity pain syndrome. Raloxifene is a selective estrogen receptor modulator (SERM).

A7: A(F) B(T) C(T) D(F) E(T)
Oral gold and hydroxychloroquine have been found to be less effective than penicillamine, intramuscular gold, methotrexate and sulphasalazine in a meta-analysis of randomised controlled trials. Thrombocytopenia associated with penicillamine therapy is a dose related phenomenon. The risk of methotrexate hepatoxicity is increased by antifolate drugs (such as cotrimoxazole), folic acid deficiency and renal impairment.

A8: A(F) B(F) C(T) D(F) E(F)
There is a 40% increased risk of abortion via the cardiolipin syndrome. Most (i.e. > 50%) children born to SLE mothers are normal, but placental transmission of maternal antibodies can cause the transient neonatal lupus syndrome with haematological and cardiac abnormalities. Chloroquine causes choroidoretinitis. The ESR rises in pregnancy anyway and disease activity is preferably measured by C_3 activity.

A9: A(T) B(F) C(F) D(T) E(F)
Pauciarticular juvenile chronic arthritis (JCA) occurs predominantly in young girls, with four or less joints affected. Affected joints are large, e.g. knees, disease is usually non-erosive. It is rheumatoid factor negative. Pauciarticular disease comprises 65% of childhood JCA. Fifty per cent

have positive antinuclear autoantibodies. Eight per cent of children with positive antinuclear autoantibodies have uveitis. Slit lamp screening is mandatory in such circumstances. Treatment is largely symptomatic using non-steroidal anti-inflammatory agents such as naproxen.

A10: A(F)   B(T)   C(T)   D(T)   E(F)

Grave's disease is an example of type V hypersensitivity (stimulatory). Acute rejection of a transplanted kidney is cell mediated hypersensitivity through T-lymphocytes.

A11: A(F)   B(T)   C(T)   D(F)   E(F)

Cell-mediated immunity reaction (type IV) are mediated by CD4 cells and independent of complement. AIDS is characterised by reduced CD4 counts and hence type IV reactions are decreased in this syndrome. Auto immune haemolytic anaemia is an example of a type II reaction.

A12: A(F)   B(T)   C(F)   D(T)   E(F)

Psoriatic arthropathy is seronegative arthropathy which usually affects the interphalangeal joints. The disease is less common in Japan. Chloroquine may exacerbate the dermatological component of the disease and therefore it should be avoided.

A13: A(F)   B(T)   C(T)   D(F)   E(T)

The serum levels of CPK are usually elevated in polymyositis–dermato-myositis complex owing to muscle damage. Involvement of proximal muscle results in waddling gait. Nikolisky's sign is a feature of pemphigus where new blisters form on applying pressure/rubbing on clinically normal skin.

A14: A(T)   B(T)   C(T)   D(T)   E(T)

A15: A(F)   B(T)   C(F)   D(F)   E(T)

Progressive systemic sclerosis is less common than SLE and has an overall five-year survival rate of 50%. The oesophagus is commonly involved by the disease process, e.g. abnormal peristalsis, reduced oesophageal sphincter pressure and strictures.

A16: A(T)   B(T)   C(T)   D(T)   E(F)

Nifedipine is a Ca^{2+} channel blocker that causes vasodilation.

A17: A(F) B(F) C(T) D(T) E(T)

The concordance rate is 30% in identical twins and 5% in non-identical twins suggesting that genes contribute to pathogenesis. Recent studies have shown an association between HLA-DR1, HLA-DR4 and seropositive disease. The pulmonary complications of RA include pleural effusion, Caplan's syndrome, fibrosing alveolitis, emphysema, rheumatoid nodules, pneumonia and obliterative bronchitis.

A18: A(F) B(F) C(T) D(F) E(T)

The serum CPK levels and EMG are usually normal in polymyalgia rheumatic, Muscle activity is usually reduced due to muscular pain. The resolution of symptoms within 72 hours of corticosteroid therapy is important in establishing the diagnosis.

Section 10

Dermatology and Genitourinary Medicine

A1:   A(T)   B(T)   C(F)   D(T)   E(F)
In keratoderma blennorhagicum, the soles are typically affected. It is seen in 10% of patients with Reiter's syndrome. In acute pompholyx, the fingers, the palms and the soles are affected with vesicular rash.

A2:   A(F)   B(T)   C(T)   D(T)   E(F)
Dermatitis herpetiformis may be associated with mild malabsorption, but gastrointestinal symptoms rarely occur. In addition to gluten free diets, dapsone or sulphapyridine may improve symptoms.

A3:   A(T)   B(T)   C(T)   D(T)   E(F)
Koebner phenomenon is the isomorphic response to scratching and trauma. Queyrat's erythroplasia is carcinoma *in situ* affecting the penis.

A4:   A(T)   B(T)   C(T)   D(F)   E(T)
The skin in rheumatoid arthritis is thin due to loss of collagen.

A5:   A(T)   B(F)   C(T)   D(T)   E(F)
The immunosuppression associated with diabetes mellitus increases the incidence of infections such as boils which are caused by *Staphylococcus aureus*. Associated hyperlipidaemia may cause xanthomata. Erythema *ab igne* is associated with hypothyroidism. Erythema marginatum is seen in rheumatic fever.

A6:   A(F)   B(T)   C(T)   D(F)   E(F)
Herpes zoster usually affects the middle aged and elderly. The disease may affect sensory and motor nerves. The disseminated form may involve various organs such as meninges and lungs.

A7:   A(F)   B(F)   C(T)   D(T)   E(T)
Common warts are caused by human papilloma viruses which are DNA
viruses. The hands and knees are usually affected.

A8:   A(F)   B(T)   C(F)   D(F)   E(F)
The male sex, old age, amelanosis, high Breslow thickness, trunk involvement and regional lymphadenopathy are poor prognostic indicators.

A9:   A(T)   B(F)   C(T)   D(T)   E(F)
Albinism is due to tyrosinase deficiency whereas lack of phenylalanine-4-
hydroxylase is the underlying abnormality in phenylketonuria. Albinism
is transmitted in an autosomal recessive fashion. The lack of melanin
causes the pale blond hair and increases the risk of melanoma.

A10:   A(T)   B(T)   C(T)   D(F)   E(F)
Protective glasses decrease the risk of cataracts. Mycosis fungoides may be
helped by PUVA.

A11:   A(T)   B(F)   C(T)   D(F)   E(T)
Cushing's syndrome and congenital adrenal hyperplasia are recognised
causes of hirsutism. Lichen planus is a condition in which the lesions are
purplish, polygonal and planar or flat topped papules. The cause is
unknown but there is an association with immunological disorders.

A12:   A(F)   B(T)   C(T)   D(T)   E(F)
Hyperhidrosis is a feature of thyrotoxicosis whereas hypohidrosis may be
seen in hypothyroidism. Pyoderma gangrenosum is a feature of inflammatory bowel disease and rheumatoid arthritis.

A13:   A(T)   B(T)   C(F)   D(F)   E(T)
Squamous cell carcinoma and syphilis are recognised causes.

A14:   A(F)   B(F)   C(F)   D(F)   E(F)
Rosacea, cold sores, athlete's foot and molloscum contagiosum may
worsen with corticosteroids.

A15:   A(F)   B(T)   C(T)   D(F)   E(T)
Tabes dorsalis and gumma are features of tertiary syphilis.

A16:   A(T)   B(T)   C(F)   D(F)   E(T)
Iron deficiency may cause koilonychia. The nail changes in psoriasis include pitting, thickening, discolouration or onycholysis.

A17:   A(F)   B(T)   C(F)   D(T)   E(T)
Tryptophan is a precursor of nicotinamide and its deficiency can lead to pellagra. In carcinoid syndrome, tryptophan is converted to 5-HT rather than to nicotamide. Very low protein diets may also lead to pellagra. There is malabsorption of tryptophan (and other amino acids) and increased loss in urine in patients with Hartnup syndrome. Isoniazid antagonises Vitamin B6 which is required for the synthesis of nicotinamide.

A18:   A(F)   B(T)   C(T)   D(F)   E(F)
Bullous pemphigoid is characterised by tense sub-epidermal blisters. The legs are usually affected. Corticosteroids and other immunosuppressants such as azathioprine are used in treatment. Pemphigus vulgaris is commonly seen in the Jewish race.

A19:   A(T)   B(T)   C(F)   D(T)   E(T)
Lowe's syndrome refers to oculocerebrorenal dystrophy with generalised amino aciduria.

A20:   A(T)   B(T)   C(T)   D(T)   E(T)

A21:   A(T)   B(T)   C(F)   D(F)   E(F)
The vesicles of chicken pox are of different ages.

A22:   A(T)   B(T)   C(F)   D(T)   E(F)
PUVA therapy may cause harm in porphyria cutanea tarda and xeroderma pigmentosum.

A23:   A(F)   B(F)   C(T)   D(T)   E(T)
Hereditary angio-oedema is inherited in an autosomal dominant fashion. The condition is due to a deficiency of C_1-esterase inhibitor.

A24:   A(F)   B(T)   C(T)   D(F)   E(F)
Antimalarial therapy and phenothiazines may cause blue/black discolouration of nails. Hypoalbuminaemia may cause white nails.

A25:   A(T)   B(T)   C(T)   D(T)   E(F)

Forrester's disease, also known as ankylosing vertebral hyperostosis, is a condition of the elderly and may be confused with ankylosing spondylitis.

A26:   A(F)   B(F)   C(T)   D(F)   E(T)

Bowen's disease and Queyrat's erythroplasia represent carcinoma in situ of the skin.

Section 11
Haematology

A1:   A(T) B(T) C(T) D(F) E(F)
Sideroblastic anaemia is an inherited or acquired disorder characterised by a refractory anaemia, hypochromic peripheral blood cells and by excessive iron and ring sideroblasts in the bone marrow. Lead can cause sideroblastic anaemia by inhibiting some enzymes involved in haem synthesis. Treatment is by withdrawal of the causative agent. Pyridoxine may help the inherited cases.

A2:   A(F) B(F) C(T) D(T) E(F)
G6PD is the most common defect of the hexose-monophosphate shunt (the most common abnormality of the Embden Myerhof pathway is pyruvate kinase deficiency). Inheritance is X-linked. Because the RBCs are unable to generate enough glutathione, they are susceptible to oxidation (e.g. by drugs, uraemia, acidosis and fava beans).

A3:   A(F) B(F) C(T) D(T) E(T)
The normal RBC lifespan is 120 days. This is reduced in haemolytic anaemia. Because the bilirubin is unconjugated, it is not filtered by glomeruli. In intravascular haemolysis, the haemoglobin is bound by haptoglobin and the resulting complex is cleared by the reticulo-endothelial system in about four minutes. When the mechanism is saturated, then haemoglobinuria occurs.

A4:   A(T) B(F) C(F) D(T) E(F)
Primary PCV requires increased red cell mass, normal PaO_2 and either splenomegaly or two of thrombocytosis, leucocytosis, raised LAP score or raised vitamin B_{12}. These secondary criteria are of course indicative of a more generalised myeloproliferative process.

A5:   A(F)   B(F)   C(F)   D(T)   E(T)
Chronic ITP arises in 10–20% of cases of acute ITP; it is defined as thrombocytopenia persisting beyond six months. Spontaneous recovery may still occur years later. Splenectomy will cure two-thirds of sufferers but at the increased risk of encapsulated organism septicaemia. It is rarely recommended for children. Temporary elevation of platelet count may be accomplished by steroids or intravenous gammaglobulin. Other therapies include: danazol, anti-rhesus D immunoglobulin, vitamin C and cytotoxic drugs. The risk of intracranial haemorrhage is less than 1%.

A6:   A(T)` B(T)   C(F)   D(F)   E(T)
Sickle cell disease often presents as one of several forms of crisis: painful, infective, sequestrative, aplastic or chest syndrome. Painful crises may initially manifest in young children as 'hands and feet' syndrome – dactylitis. Sequestration, particularly splenic, occurs in infancy with acute splenomegaly. However recurrent splenic infarcts cause 'autosplenectomisation' with the absence of a palpable spleen in early childhood. Infective crises may be caused by unusual organisms. Osteomyelitis due to salmonella is well recorded. Disease affecting the renal medulla and consequently the concentrating power of the kidneys, gives rise to nocturnal enuresis. Haemosiderotic cardiomyopathy is a feature of haematological disorders requiring multiple transfusions and subsequent iron overload such as B thalassaemia.

A7:   A(F)   B(F)   C(T)   D(T)   E(F)
The detection of IgM antibodies (cold) is carried out at room temperature. The indirect Coomb's test is used for this purpose. Group O rhesus negative blood should be transfused in emergencies.

A8:   A(T)   B(T)   C(T)   D(F)   E(T)
There is fibrinogen deficiency.

A9:   A(T)   B(F)   C(T)   D(F)   E(T)
The antibody (IgG) can cross the placenta causing neonatal thrombocytopenia. Then splenectomy can be safely performed. Following splenectomy, the long-term remission rate is about 70% of cases, due to the presence of the antibody.

A10:   A(T)   B(F)   C(F)   D(T)   E(T)
Bleeding time can be prolonged in conditions associated with a low count

or dysfunction of the platelets.

A11: A(F) B(T) C(T) D(T) E(F)
In haemophilia A, the level of factor VIII:C is reduced but the level of factor VIII:vWF is normal. The gene causing the disease was cloned in 1984. It occupies 0.1% of the X-chromosome (186 kb). The bleeding and prothrombin times are normal.

A12: A(T) B(T) C(T) D(T) E(F)
PTTK is sensitive to factors in the intrinsic and common pathways.

A13: A(T) B(T) C(T) D(T) E(F)

A14: A(T) B(F) C(T) D(T) E(F)
Renal impairment is present in 15–20% of patients who present with myeloma. It often improves with high fluid intake. The single most important prognostic factor is the serum level of B_2-microglobulin at diagnosis. There is some evidence to suggest that combination chemotherapy has advantages over intermittent melphalan with respect to long term survival.

A15: A(T) B(F) C(T) D(F) E(F)
The cervical lymph nodes are most commonly involved at presentation. The involvement of non-lymphatic tissue (e.g. skin, lung, brain, etc) usually occurs late. Radiotherapy is the treatment of choice for stages I and II.

A16: A(F) B(T) C(T) D(F) E(T)
The ferritin is usually reduced. The TIBC rises as the saturation decreases due to iron deficiency.

A17: A(T) B(F) C(F) D(F) E(T)
In the neonate, vitamin K deficiency is usually due to absence of bacteria in the foetal gut able to synthesise vitamin K. Menandione is a water-soluble form which can be absorbed in the absence of bile salts. Factors II, VII, IX and X undergo decarboxylation in the presence of vitamin K. It takes about 12–20 hours to reverse warfarin anticoagulation.

A18: A(T) B(F) C(F) D(T) E(T)
The fact that erythropoietin activity persists after bilateral nephrectomy suggests another source of erythropoietin production, such as the liver. Erythropoietin decreases the maturation time of red blood cell precursors. The elevated level of haemoglobin in PRV causes a reduction in erythropoietin production via negative feedback mechanisms.

A19: A(F) B(F) C(T) D(F) E(T)
CLL does not occur in children and it is rare in young adults. The incidence rises rapidly with advancing age. It usually presents with lymphadenopathy with or without splenomegaly. Some early cases are diagnosed incidentally on a blood count performed for other reasons. In over 95% of cases, the lymphocytes are B-cells which express low levels of restricted light-chain surface immunoglobulins. Treatment is only indicated in symptomatic patients. Poor prognostic indicators include splenomegaly, bone marrow failure and a high prolymphocytosis at presentation.

A20: A(T) B(F) C(F) D(F) E(T)
Poor prognostic indicators in ALL include male sex, high peripheral white count at presentation, age less than 2 years or over 10 years at presentation, certain chromosomal abnormalities, morphological L3 and L2 subtypes and immunological null-ALL, B-ALL and T-ALL subtypes.

A21: A(F) B(T) C(F) D(F) E(T)
Most patients have low serum erythropoietin levels. This finding is important in supporting the diagnosis of primary polycythaemia. The platelet and white cell counts may be raised initially. This is also true of secondary polycythaemia.

A22: A(T) B(T) C(F) D(F) E(T)
Other familial thrombophilic syndromes include protein S deficiency and antithrombin deficiency. Antiphospholipid and Behçet's syndromes are acquired prethrombotic conditions. The indications for thrombophilia screening include venous thromboembolism presenting before the age of 45 years, recurrent venous thrombosis, venous thrombosis in an unusual anatomical site and positive family history of thrombophilia.

Section 12

Medical Microbiology

A1:   A(T)   B(F)   C(F)   D(F)   E(T)
Klebsiella penumoniae is a Gram-negative rod. It is carried in the respiratory tract of 10% of normal people and causes a clinical infection if the host defences are compromised by age or disease (eg diabetes and advanced cancer). It may cause a UTI in patients with indwelling urinary catheters. The organism is resistant to amoxycillin. Aminoglycosides, cephalosporins and erythromycin may be used in treatment empirically. The choice of drug depends however on the results of sensitivity as hospital-acquired organisms are frequently resistant to multiple antibiotics.

A2:   A(T)   B(T)   C(T)   D(F)   E(F)
Leptospirosis is usually contracted through the skin and legionnaire's disease is transmitted by airborne particles.

A3:   A(T)   B(F)   C(T)   D(T)   E(F)
The clinical features of *F. malaria* include convulsions, anaemia, fever, renal failure, acute respiratory distress syndrome, thrombocytopenia, hypoglycaemia and DIC. The side effects of mefloquine include psychiatric disturbance and teratogenicity. Thrombocytopenia is universal in patients with *F. malaria*. Prevention measures include adequate travel advice, use of insect repellents, wearing long sleeves at night and chemoprophylaxis.

A4:   A(F)   B(T)   C(T)   D(T)   E(F)
Lyme disease is the most commonly reported vector-borne disease in the USA. It is transmitted by Ixodes ticks. The disease is caused by the spirochaete *Borrelia burgdorferi*. Tetracycline, cephalosporin and penicillin are effective in the treatment of stage I disease. However, despite treatment, the disease progresses to stage II and/or stage III in 1% of patients. Serological tests are used for diagnosis and PCR has been recently

introduced. Other clinical features include fever, skin rashes, myalgia, arthritis and encephalopathy.

A5:   A(T)   B(F)   C(T)   D(F)   E(F)

Pseudomembranous colitis can be caused by a wide variety of antibiotics such as ampicillin and clindamycin. It causes diarrhoea. The condition can be diagnosed by demonstrating the cytotoxic effects of the toxin on cultured cells. Sigmoidoscopy may reveal pseudomembranous plaques (white-yellow) which can be biopsied. It is treated by fluid replacement and oral metronidazole or vancomycin. The causative drug is withdrawn.

A6:   A(F)   B(T)   C(F)   D(T)   E(T)

In the Mantoux test, the PPD is injected intradermally. The test is considered positive if a 10 mm area of induration (and erythema) develops 48–72 hours after the injection. The test is usually positive in patients with a previous history of BCG vaccine or TB infection. The test is usually positive during active infection and takes 4–6 weeks to become positive in infected patients. The skin test is a delayed hypersensitivity reaction (type IV) and is impaired in patients with depleted CD4 cells, e.g. patients with AIDS.

A7:   A(T)   B(F)   C(T)   D(F)   E(F)

S. aureus is a Gram-positive coccus. The colonies appear golden yellow (colour ranges from white to orange). It is coagulase and phosphatase positive. Lancefield classification applies to streptococci.

A8:   A(T)   B(T)   C(F)   D(T)   E(T)

Endotoxins are weakly antigenic lipopolysaccharides that can cause fever and shock. The fever is due to the action of interleukin-1 on the hypothalamus. IL-1 is released by macrophage due to the effect of endotoxins. Bradykinin-induced vasodilatation and increased vascular permeability can lead to shock. Other effects of endotoxins include DIC due to activation of factor XII, activation of alternative complement pathway and activation of macrophages and B-lymphocytes. These biological effects of endotoxins are mediated by cytokines namely IL-1 and tumour necrosis factor.

A9:   A(T)   B(T)   C(F)   D(T)   E(F)

H. pylori is a Gram-negative organism that is implicated in peptic ulceration. It is also associated with gastric cancer and chronic active gastritis. It is found in the antrum more frequently than the body and it is often detected in the gastric mucosa of Meckel's diverticulum. *H. pylori* infection may be diagnosed with endoscopic biopsy, serum antibodies, titres or breath tests. The organism is sensitive to metronidazole, clarithromycin and amoxycillin.

A10: A(F)   B(T)   C(F)   D(T)   E(T)

H. influenzae is a Gram-negative bacillus. It requires factor X (haemin) and V (NAD) for its growth. *H. influenzae* causes pneumonia in the elderly, meningitis in young children, otitis media, sinusitis and epiglottis. The organism is sensitive to cephalosporins, ampicillin and ciprofloxacin.

Section 13
Genetic Statistics and Molecular Biology

A1:   A(T)   B(T)   C(T)   D(T)   E(T)

Other conditions seen more frequently in Down's syndrome include congenital heart disease, growth retardation, hypotonicity, hyperkeratotic skin, vitiligo, hypermetropia, deafness, duodenal atresia, leukaemia, epilepsy and early dementia.

A2:   A(T)   B(F)   C(F)   D(T)   E(F)

The important thing to remember is than non-parametric tests are required where the distributions are not normal (Gaussian). There is often one statistics question in MRCP part 1

A3:   A(T)   B(F)   C(F)   D(T)   E(T)

The cystic fibrosis gene comprises 250 kilobases on chromosome 7q. The gene product, a polypeptide of 1480 amino acids is termed the cystic fibrosis transmembrane regulator. The most common gene mutation (68% of northern European patients) codes for a phenylalanine deletion at position 508. This may be detected using the polymerase chain reaction. Severe pancreatic insufficiency is correlated with the homozygous F508 genotype.

A4:   A(T)   B(F)   C(T)   D(T)   E(T)

There are may causes of a false positive sweat test including adrenal insufficiency, flucloxacillin therapy, ectodermal dysplasia, nephrogenic diabetes insipidus, hypothyroidism, glycogen storage disease type I and mucopolysaccharidoses. Normal subjects have sweat tests with sodium content above that of the chloride concentration.

A5:   A(F)   B(F)   C(T)   D(F)   E(T)

The gene is located on autosomes. An example of exception is neuro-fibromatosis where there is a high spontaneous mutation rate and on the short arm of chromosome 6.

A6:   A(T)   B(T)   C(T)   D(F)   E(F)

Specimens from mammoths have been analysed. A growing number of genetically determined diseases can be diagnosed with PCR (including muscular dystrophy). False positive results can be obtained if similar sequences occur in unrelated nucleic acids. The main virtue of the technique is that, because it amplifies, only a small specimen is required. For this reason, it is not a good test for malaria when chronic low-grade parasitaemia is common in endemic areas.

A7:   A(F)   B(T)   C(F)   D(F)   E(T)

It is a parametric statistical test. The larger the sample size, the closer the distribution to normal and for each number of degrees of freedom, there is a completely critical ratio.

A8:   A(T)   B(T)   C(F)   D(T)   E(F)

The SEM assesses the reliability of the mean and it is related to the SD:

$$SEM = \frac{SD}{n}$$

Since n is always greater than 1, the SEM is always smaller than the SD.

A9:   A(F)   B(T)   C(F)   D(T)   E(F)

In a normal distribution, the mean, mode and median coincide. 68% of observations lie within 1 SD of the mean, 95% within 2.5 SDs and 99% within 2.6 SDs. The co-efficient of variation V_{var} measures the spread of values and is given by:

$$V_{var} = \frac{SD}{Mean} \times 100$$

A10:   A(T)   B(F)   C(T)   D(F)   E(T)

The power of the trial equals type II error. Type I error describes the probability of accepting a null hypothesis (Ho) when it is in fact invalid, i.e. the probability of false positives. The number of patients required for the trial depends upon type I and type II errors and the minimal relevant difference.

A11: A(T) B(F) C(T) D(F) E(T)
The haemoccult test detects three cancers per 1000 persons screened. The false positive rate is 25% and this is usually due to various dietary factors such as carrots and red meat. The addition of a peroxidase inhibitor may increase the test accuracy.

A12: A(T) B(T) C(F) D(F) E(T)
Audit is composed of three components: audit of structure (e.g. staffing levels), audit of process (e.g. the way the patient is management from admission till discharge) and audit of outcome (e.g. morbidity, mortality and QALYs). Audit demands confidentiality to both patients and clinical participants. It is an educational exercise aimed at improving standards.

A13: A(F) B(F) C(F) D(T) E(T)
Phenyketonuria and Dubin–Johnson syndrome are transmitted by autosomal recessive inheritance. The inheritance of Duchenne muscular dystrophy is X-linked.

A14: A(F) B(F) C(T) D(T) E(F)
Patients with Klinefelter's syndrome have an XXY genotype. This results in small penis and testicles. There may be female breast development and reduced libido. Homosexuality and transvestism are common. A, B and E are true of Turner's syndrome.

A15: A(T) B(F) C(T) D(T) E(F)
Von Gierke's disease results from a genetically determined deficiency of glucose-6-phosphotase. Hypoglycaemia is a feature of the disease, therefore management involves a special diet to maintain the level of blood glucose. Wilson's disease is treated with a low copper diet and D-penicillamine. A diet free from phenylalanine can prevent the severe complications of phenylketonuria.

A16:   A(F)   B(T)   C(F)   D(F)   E(T)
Cystic fibrosis is inherited in an autosomal recessive fashion (chromosome 5). The inheritance of Huntingdon's chorea is autosomal dominant.

A17:   A(F)   B(T)   C(T)   D(F)   E(F)
Exons are the coding sequences of genes. The role of the non-coding sequences known as *introns* remains unclear. Reverse transcriptase is the enzyme used by retroviruses to construct DNA. PCR refers to DNA amplification by chemical proliferation rather than by biologic proliferation in a host cell which is known as molecular cloning.

A18:   A(F)   B(F)   C(F)   D(T)   E(T)
The results of the above study can be summarised in the 2×2 contingency table (Table 1).

Table 1.   Telomerase activity in 14 human breast cancers (observed frequencies)

Telomerase	Node positive	Node negative	Total
Positive	7	3	10
Negative	0	8	8
Total	7	11	18

Table 2.   Expected frequencies of Table 1

Telomerase	Node positive	Node negative	Total
Positive	3.9	6.1	10
Negative	3.1	4.9	8
Total	7	11	18

It can also be seen from Table 2 that the sample is small and only one of the expected frequencies exceeds 5. Therefore a standard chi-squared test is inappropriate. Fisher's exact test and the chi-squared test with Yate's correction can be used for comparing the groups. McNemar's test is appropriate for matched samples.

Note that one of the observed frequencies is zero. Hence the number of degrees of freedom for this table is

$$(2 - 1) \times (2 - 1) = 1$$

The corrected chi-squared statistic for a 2 × 2 table is

$$\sum \frac{[(\text{Observed frequency} - \text{Expected frequency}) - 0.5]^2}{\text{Expected frequency}}$$

In the above study, the chi-square statistic with Yate's correction is 6.455, giving a *p*-value of 0.011. The Fisher's exact test also gives a *p*-value smaller than the critical value of 0.05.

A19:   A(T)   B(T)   C(T)   D(F)   E(F)

For interval data, if the sample is large then the normal distribution test is most appropriate. If the sample is small and the distribution of differences is normal, then the paired test is appropriate. For small samples and non-normal distribution, Wilcoxon matched pairs test can be used. Sign test is also suitable for ordered nominal data.

A20:   A(F)   B(T)   C(F)   D(T)   E(T)

The normal distribution for means is suitable for interval data and large samples. Chi-squared for trend is appropriate for nominal ordered data and samples exceeding 30. Dichotomous data with small samples and expected frequencies < 5 can be compared using Fisher's exact test or chi-squared test with Yate's correction. Standard chi-squared test is appropriate for dichotomous data and large samples (80% of expected frequencies exceed 5).

A21:   A(F)   B(F)   C(T)   D(T)   E(F)

When the one sample *t*-test is used with differences, it is known as paired *t*-test. The test is based on the normal distribution and is suitable for small samples.

A22:   A(T)   B(F)   C(F)   D(F)   E(F)

The number of degrees of freedom is given by

(Number of rows – 1) × (Number of columns – 1)

The chi-squared test is valid if at least 80% of the expected frequencies exceed 5 and all the expected frequencies exceed 1. The observed

frequencies can be zero. In our example, at least five expected frequencies
(0.8×6) must exceed 5.

A23:   A(T)   B(F)   C(F)   D(F)   E(T)

Fisher's exact test which applies to 2×2 tables is suitable for small
samples with small expected frequencies. It usually gives a large probability than the standard chi-squared test. The latter is more suitable
when the expected frequencies are large. Fisher's exact test is more
difficult to calculate when the expected frequencies are large, since the
factorials of these large numbers require calculation.

Section 14

Thermoregulation

A1:   A(F)   B(F)   C(T)   D(F)   E(F)

Hypothermia occurs when the core body temperature falls below 35°C. The causes include hypothyroidism (5%), hypopituitarism, alcoholism, phenothiazines, pneumonia and benzodiazepines. Inability to shiver in response to cold may be the causative mechanism, hence increased muscle tone and neck stiffness and are recognised features. The condition may cause sinus bradycardia, prolonged PR interval, junctional (J) wave and/or ventricular fibrillation. Tissue hypoxia may cause a metabolic acidosis. Treatment includes surface rewarming (0.5°C/h), oxygen, fluids and/or positive pressure ventilation. The underlying cause should be corrected and i.v. T_3 is indicated in hypothyroidism. The delta wave is a feature of Wolff–Parkinson–White syndrome.

A2:   A(T)   B(F)   C(T)   D(F)   E(T)

Spinal cord injury and barbiturates are recognised causes of hypothermia. Seizures and exercise increase heat production by increasing muscle activity.

A3:   A(T)   B(T)   C(F)   D(T)   E(F)

Diuresis is due to a central shift in the blood volume, impaired tubular function and reduced responsiveness to ADH. Dantrolene is used in the treatment of hyperthermia. Salicylates uncouple oxidative phosphorylation.

A4:   A(F)   B(T)   C(T)   D(T)   E(T)

Other ECG changes include widened QRS, complex atrial flutter, atrial fibrillation, sinus bradycardia and ST changes. The J wave is seen at the junction of QRS and ST segments.